R Programming

Copyright © 2019 by **R Publishing**

R - A Beginner's Guide

R is an open source programming language and software environment for statistical computing. The R language is widely used among statisticians and data miners for developing statistical software and data analysis.

R is an implementation of the S programming language. The R language came to use quite a bit after S had been developed. One key limitation of the S language was that it was only available in a commercial package, S-PLUS. In 1991, R was created by Ross Ihaka and Robert Gentleman in the Department of Statistics at the University of Auckland. In 1993 the first announcement of R was made to the public.

A major advantage that R has over many other statistical packages and is that it's free in the sense of free software. R is both flexible and powerful. It has an amazing ecosystem for developers and It has wide range of packages for data access, data cleaning or munging, performing Analysis, creating Reports etc.

The primary R system is available from the Comprehensive R Archive Network, also known as CRAN. CRAN also hosts many add-on packages that can be used to extend the functionality of R. Over 6,789 packages are available on CRAN that have been developed by users and programmers around the world.

This tutorial helps you to build your base with R.

To whom this tutorial is designed for:

This book is designed for software programmers, statisticians and data miners who are looking forward for developing statistical software using R programming. If you are trying to understand the R programming language as a beginner, this book will give you enough understanding on almost all the concepts of the language from where you can take yourself to higher levels of expertise.

Prerequisites:

Before proceeding with this book, you should have a basic understanding of Computer Programming terminologies. A basic understanding of any of the programming languages will help you in understanding the R programming concepts and move fast on the learning track.

Table of Contents

R - Introduction

R is a programming language and software environment for statistical analysis, graphics representation and reporting. R was created by Ross Ihaka and Robert Gentleman at the University of Auckland, New Zealand, and is currently developed by the R Development Core Team.

The core of R is an interpreted computer language which allows branching and looping as well as modular programming using functions. R allows integration with the procedures written in the C, C++, .Net, Python or FORTRAN languages for efficiency.

R is freely available under the GNU General Public License, and pre-compiled binary versions are provided for various operating systems like Linux, Windows and Mac.

R is free software distributed under a GNU-style copy left, and an official part of the GNU project called **GNU S**.

Evolution of R:

R was initially written by **Ross Ihaka** and **Robert Gentleman** at the Department of Statistics of the University of Auckland in Auckland, New Zealand. R made its first appearance in 1993.

- A large group of individuals has contributed to R by sending code and bug reports.

- Since mid-1997 there has been a core group (the "R Core Team") who can modify the R source code archive.

Features of R:

As stated earlier, R is a programming language and software environment for statistical analysis, graphics representation and reporting. The following are the important features of R –

- R is a well-developed, simple and effective programming language which includes conditionals, loops, user defined recursive functions and input and output facilities.

- R has an effective data handling and storage facility,

- R provides a suite of operators for calculations on arrays, lists, vectors and matrices.

- R provides a large, coherent and integrated collection of tools for data analysis.

- R provides graphical facilities for data analysis and display either directly at the computer or printing at the papers.

As a conclusion, R is world's most widely used statistics programming language. It's the # 1 choice of data scientists and supported by a vibrant and talented community of contributors. R is taught in universities and deployed in mission critical business applications. This tutorial will teach you R programming along with suitable examples in simple and easy steps.

R - Environment Setup

Local Environment Setup:

If you are still willing to set up your environment for R, you can follow the steps given below.

Windows Installation:

You can download the Windows installer version of R from R-3.2.2 for Windows (32/64 bit) and save it in a local directory.

As it is a Windows installer (.exe) with a name "R-version-win.exe". You can just double click and run the installer accepting the default settings. If your Windows is 32-bit version, it installs the 32-bit version. But if your windows is 64-bit, then it installs both the 32-bit and 64-bit versions.

After installation you can locate the icon to run the Program in a directory structure "R\R3.2.2\bin\i386\Rgui.exe" under the Windows Program Files. Clicking this icon brings up the R-GUI which is the R console to do R Programming.

Linux Installation:

R is available as a binary for many versions of Linux at the location R Binaries.

The instruction to install Linux varies from flavor to flavor. These steps are mentioned under each type of Linux version in the mentioned link. However, if you are in a hurry, then you can use **yum** command to install R as follows −

```
$ yum install R
```

Above command will install core functionality of R programming along with standard packages, still you need additional package, then you can launch R prompt as follows −

```
$ R
R version 3.6.1 (2019-08-30) -- "Full of Ingredients"
Copyright (C) 2019 The R Foundation for Statistical Computing
Platform: x86_64-redhat-linux-gnu (64-bit)
```

R is free software and comes with ABSOLUTELY NO WARRANTY.
You are welcome to redistribute it under certain conditions.
Type 'license()' or 'licence()' for distribution details.

R is a collaborative project with many contributors.
Type 'contributors()' for more information and
'citation()' on how to cite R or R packages in publications.

Type 'demo()' for some demos, 'help()' for on-line help, or
'help.start()' for an HTML browser interface to help.
Type 'q()' to quit R.
>

Now you can use install command at R prompt to install the required package. For example, the following command will install **plotrix** package which is required for 3D charts.

```
> install.packages("plotrix")
```

R - Basic Syntax

As a convention, we will start learning R programming by writing a "Hello, World!" program. Depending on the needs, you can program either at R command prompt or you can use an R script file to write your program. Let's check both one by one.

R Command Prompt:

Once you have R environment setup, then it's easy to start your R command prompt by just typing the following command at your command prompt −

```
$ R
```

This will launch R interpreter and you will get a prompt > where you can start typing your program as follows −

```
> myString <- "Hello, World!"
> print ( myString)
[1] "Hello, World!"
```

Here first statement defines a string variable myString, where we assign a string "Hello, World!" and then next statement print() is being used to print the value stored in variable myString.

R Script File:

Usually, you will do your programming by writing your programs in script files and then you execute those scripts at your command prompt with the help of R interpreter called **Rscript**. So let's start with writing following code in a text file called test.R as under –

```
# My first program in R Programming
myString <- "Hello, World!"

print ( myString)
```

Save the above code in a file test.R and execute it at Linux command prompt as given below. Even if you are using Windows or other system, syntax will remain same.

```
$ Rscript test.R
```

When we run the above program, it produces the following result.

```
[1] "Hello, World!"
```

Comments:

Comments are like helping text in your R program and they are ignored by the interpreter while executing your actual program. Single comment is written using # in the beginning of the statement as follows –

```
# My first program in R Programming
```

R does not support multi-line comments but you can perform a trick which is something as follows –

```
if(FALSE) {
   "This is a demo for multi-line comments and it should be
put inside either a
```

```
      single OR double quote"
}

myString <- "Hello, World!"
print ( myString)


[1] "Hello, World!"
```

Though above comments will be executed by R interpreter, they will not interfere with your actual program. You should put such comments inside, either single or double quote.

R - Data Types

Generally, while doing programming in any programming language, you need to use various variables to store various information. Variables are nothing but reserved memory locations to store values. This means that, when you create a variable you reserve some space in memory.

You may like to store information of various data types like character, wide character, integer, floating point, double floating point, Boolean etc. Based on the data type of a variable, the operating system allocates memory and decides what can be stored in the reserved memory.

In contrast to other programming languages like C and java in R, the variables are not declared as some data type. The variables are assigned with R-Objects and the data type of the R-object becomes the data type of the variable. There are many types of R-objects. The frequently used ones are −

- Vectors
- Lists
- Matrices
- Arrays
- Factors
- Data Frames

The simplest of these objects is the **vector object** and there are six data types of these atomic vectors, also termed as six classes of vectors. The other R-Objects are built upon the atomic vectors.

Data Type	Example	Verify

Logical	TRUE, FALSE	```v <- TRUE```
		```print(class(v))```
		
		it produces the following result −
		
		[1] "logical"

Numeric	12.3, 5, 999	```v <- 23.5```
		```print(class(v))```
		
		it produces the following result −
		
		[1] "numeric"

Integer	2L, 34L, 0L	```v <- 2L```
		```print(class(v))```
		
		it produces the following result −
		
		[1] "integer"

Complex	3 + 2i	```v <- 2+5i```
		```print(class(v))```
		
		it produces the following result −
		
		[1] "complex"

Character	'a' , "'good", "TRUE",	```v <- "TRUE"``` ```print(class(v))```

	'23.4'	it produces the following result – [1] "character"
Raw	"Hello" is stored as 48 65 6c 6c 6f	v <-charToRaw("Hello") print(class(v)) it produces the following result – [1] "raw"

In R programming, the very basic data types are the R-objects called **vectors** which hold elements of different classes as shown above. Please note in R the number of classes is not confined to only the above six types. For example, we can use many atomic vectors and create an array whose class will become array.

Vectors:

When you want to create vector with more than one element, you should use **c()**function which means to combine the elements into a vector.

```
# Create a vector.
apple <- c('red','green',"yellow")
print(apple)

# Get the class of the vector.
print(class(apple))
```

When we execute the above code, it produces the following result −

```
[1] "red"    "green" "yellow"
[1] "character"
```

Lists:

A list is an R-object which can contain many different types of elements inside it like vectors, functions and even another list inside it.

```
# Create a list.
list1 <- list(c(2,5,3),21.3,sin)

# Print the list.
print(list1)
```

When we execute the above code, it produces the following result −

```
[[1]]
[1] 2 5 3

[[2]]
[1] 21.3

[[3]]
function (x) .Primitive("sin")
```

Matrices:

A matrix is a two-dimensional rectangular data set. It can be created using a vector input to the matrix function.

```
# Create a matrix.
M = matrix( c('a','a','b','c','b','a'), nrow = 2, ncol = 3, byrow = TRUE)
print(M)
```

When we execute the above code, it produces the following result −

```
     [,1] [,2] [,3]
[1,] "a"  "a"  "b"
[2,] "c"  "b"  "a"
```

Arrays:

While matrices are confined to two dimensions, arrays can be of any number of dimensions. The array function takes a dim attribute which creates the required number of dimension. In the below example we create an array with two elements which are 3x3 matrices each.

```
# Create an array.
a <- array(c('green','yellow'),dim = c(3,3,2))
print(a)
```

When we execute the above code, it produces the following result −

```
, , 1

     [,1]    [,2]    [,3]
[1,] "green"  "yellow" "green"
[2,] "yellow" "green"  "yellow"
[3,] "green"  "yellow" "green"


, , 2

     [,1]     [,2]    [,3]
[1,] "yellow" "green"  "yellow"
[2,] "green"  "yellow" "green"
[3,] "yellow" "green"  "yellow"
```

Factors:

Factors are the r-objects which are created using a vector. It stores the vector along with the distinct values of the elements in the vector as labels. The labels are always character irrespective of whether it is numeric or character or Boolean etc. in the input vector. They are useful in statistical modeling.

Factors are created using the **factor()** function. The **nlevels** functions gives the count of levels.

```
# Create a vector.
apple_colors                                                    <-
c('green','green','yellow','red','red','red','green')

# Create a factor object.
factor_apple <- factor(apple_colors)

# Print the factor.
print(factor_apple)
```

```
print(nlevels(factor_apple))
```

When we execute the above code, it produces the following result −

```
[1] green green yellow red   red   red   green
Levels: green red yellow
[1] 3
```

Data Frames:

Data frames are tabular data objects. Unlike a matrix in data frame each column can contain different modes of data. The first column can be numeric while the second column can be character and third column can be logical. It is a list of vectors of equal length.

Data Frames are created using the **data.frame()** function.

```
# Create the data frame.
BMI <-   data.frame(
  gender = c("Male", "Male","Female"),
  height = c(152, 171.5, 165),
  weight = c(81,93, 78),
  Age = c(42,38,26)
)
print(BMI)
```

When we execute the above code, it produces the following result −

```
  gender height weight Age
1 Male   152.0   81   42
2 Male   171.5   93   38
3 Female 165.0   78   26
```

R - Variables

A variable provides us with named storage that our programs can manipulate. A variable in R can store an atomic vector, group of atomic vectors or a combination of many Robjects. A valid variable name consists of letters, numbers and the dot or underline characters. The variable name starts with a letter or the dot not followed by a number.

Variable Name	Validity	Reason
var_name2.	valid	Has letters, numbers, dot and underscore
var_name%	Invalid	Has the character '%'. Only dot(.) and underscore allowed.
2var_name	invalid	Starts with a number
.var_name, var.name	valid	Can start with a dot(.) but the dot(.)should not be followed by a number.
.2var_name	invalid	The starting dot is followed by a

		number making it invalid.
_var_name	invalid	Starts with _ which is not valid

Variable Assignment:

The variables can be assigned values using leftward, rightward and equal to operator. The values of the variables can be printed using **print()** or **cat()** function. The **cat()**function combines multiple items into a continuous print output.

```
# Assignment using equal operator.
var.1 = c(0,1,2,3)

# Assignment using leftward operator.
var.2 <- c("learn","R")

# Assignment using rightward operator.
c(TRUE,1) -> var.3

print(var.1)
cat ("var.1 is ", var.1 ,"\n")
cat ("var.2 is ", var.2 ,"\n")
cat ("var.3 is ", var.3 ,"\n")
```

When we execute the above code, it produces the following result –

```
[1] 0 1 2 3
var.1 is  0 1 2 3
var.2 is  learn R
var.3 is  1 1
```

Note – The vector c(TRUE,1) has a mix of logical and numeric class. So logical class is coerced to numeric class making TRUE as 1.

Data Type of a Variable:

In R, a variable itself is not declared of any data type, rather it gets the data type of the R - object assigned to it. So R is called a dynamically typed language, which means that we can change a variable's data type of the same variable again and again when using it in a program.

```
var_x <- "Hello"
cat("The class of var_x is ",class(var_x),"\n")

var_x <- 34.5
cat(" Now the class of var_x is ",class(var_x),"\n")

var_x <- 27L
cat(" Next the class of var_x becomes ",class(var_x),"\n")
```

When we execute the above code, it produces the following result –

```
The class of var_x is  character
 Now the class of var_x is  numeric
  Next the class of var_x becomes  integer
```

Finding Variables:

To know all the variables currently available in the workspace we use the **ls()** function. Also the ls() function can use patterns to match the variable names.

```
print(ls())
```

When we execute the above code, it produces the following result –

```
[1] "my var"    "my_new_var" "my_var"    "var.1"
[5] "var.2"     "var.3"     "var.name"  "var_name2."
[9] "var_x"     "varname"
```

Note – It is a sample output depending on what variables are declared in your environment.

The ls() function can use patterns to match the variable names.

```
# List the variables starting with the pattern "var".
print(ls(pattern = "var"))
```

When we execute the above code, it produces the following result –

```
[1] "my var"    "my_new_var" "my_var"    "var.1"
[5] "var.2"     "var.3"     "var.name"  "var_name2."
[9] "var_x"     "varname"
```

The variables starting with **dot(.)** are hidden, they can be listed using "all.names = TRUE" argument to ls() function.

```
print(ls(all.name = TRUE))
```

When we execute the above code, it produces the following result −

```
[1] ".cars"      ".Random.seed" ".var_name"   ".varname"
".varname2"
[6] "my var"      "my_new_var"  "my_var"       "var.1"
"var.2"
[11]"var.3"      "var.name"    "var_name2." "var_x"
```

Deleting Variables:

Variables can be deleted by using the **rm()** function. Below we delete the variable var.3. On printing the value of the variable error is thrown.

```
rm(var.3)
print(var.3)
```

When we execute the above code, it produces the following result −

```
[1] "var.3"
Error in print(var.3) : object 'var.3' not found
```

All the variables can be deleted by using the **rm()** and **ls()** function together.

```
rm(list = ls())
print(ls())
```

When we execute the above code, it produces the following result −

```
character(0)
```

R - Operators

An operator is a symbol that tells the compiler to perform specific mathematical or logical manipulations. R language is rich in built-in operators and provides following types of operators.

Types of Operators:

We have the following types of operators in R programming –

- Arithmetic Operators
- Relational Operators
- Logical Operators
- Assignment Operators
- Miscellaneous Operators

Arithmetic Operators:

Following table shows the arithmetic operators supported by R language. The operators act on each element of the vector.

Operator	Description	Example
+	Adds two vectors	v <- c(2,5.5,6) t <- c(8, 3, 4) print(v+t)
		it produces the

		following result –
		[1] 10.0 8.5 10.0
–	Subtracts second vector from the first	```v <- c(2,5.5,6)
t <- c(8, 3, 4)
print(v-t)```
		it produces the following result –
		[1] -6.0 2.5 2.0
*	Multiplies both vectors	```v <- c(2,5.5,6)
t <- c(8, 3, 4)
print(v*t)```
		it produces the following result –
		[1] 16.0 16.5 24.0
/	Divide the first vector with the second	```v <- c(2,5.5,6)
t <- c(8, 3, 4)
print(v/t)```
		When we execute the above code, it produces the following result –
		[1] 0.250000 1.833333 1.500000
%%	Give the remainder	```v <- c(2,5.5,6)
t <- c(8, 3, 4)```

	of the first vector with the second	print(v%%t) it produces the following result – [1] 2.0 2.5 2.0
%/%	The result of division of first vector with second (quotient)	v <- c(2,5.5,6) t <- c(8, 3, 4) print(v%/%t) it produces the following result – [1] 0 1 1
^	The first vector raised to the exponent of second vector	v <- c(2,5.5,6) t <- c(8, 3, 4) print(v^t) it produces the following result – [1] 256.000 166.375 1296.000

Relational Operators:

Following table shows the relational operators supported by R language. Each element of the first vector is compared with the corresponding element of the second vector. The result of comparison is a Boolean value.

Operator	Description	Example

>	Checks if each element of the first vector is greater than the corresponding element of the second vector.	`v <- c(2,5.5,6,9)`
		`t <- c(8,2.5,14,9)`
		`print(v>t)`
		
		it produces the following result −
		
		`[1] FALSE TRUE FALSE FALSE`

<	Checks if each element of the first vector is less than the corresponding element of the second vector.	`v <- c(2,5.5,6,9)`
		`t <- c(8,2.5,14,9)`
		`print(v < t)`
		
		it produces the following result −
		
		`[1] TRUE FALSE TRUE FALSE`

==	Checks if each element of the first vector is equal to the corresponding element of the second vector.	`v <- c(2,5.5,6,9)`
		`t <- c(8,2.5,14,9)`
		`print(v == t)`
		
		it produces the following result −
		
		`[1] FALSE FALSE FALSE TRUE`

<=	Checks if each element of the first vector is less than or equal to	`v <- c(2,5.5,6,9)`
		`t <- c(8,2.5,14,9)`
		`print(v<=t)`

	the corresponding element of the second vector.	it produces the following result – [1] TRUE FALSE TRUE TRUE
>=	Checks if each element of the first vector is greater than or equal to the corresponding element of the second vector.	v <- c(2,5.5,6,9) t <- c(8,2.5,14,9) print(v>=t) it produces the following result – [1] FALSE TRUE FALSE TRUE
!=	Checks if each element of the first vector is unequal to the corresponding element of the second vector.	v <- c(2,5.5,6,9) t <- c(8,2.5,14,9) print(v!=t) it produces the following result – [1] TRUE TRUE TRUE FALSE

Logical Operators:

Following table shows the logical operators supported by R language. It is applicable only to vectors of type logical, numeric or complex. All numbers greater than 1 are considered as logical value TRUE.

Each element of the first vector is compared with the corresponding element of the second vector. The result of comparison is a Boolean value.

Operator	Description	Example
&	It is called Element-wise Logical AND operator. It combines each element of the first vector with the corresponding element of the second vector and gives a output TRUE if both the elements are TRUE.	```\nv <-\nc(3,1,TRUE,2+3i)\nt <-\nc(4,1,FALSE,2+3i)\nprint(v&t)\n``` it produces the following result – [1] TRUE TRUE FALSE TRUE
|	It is called Element-wise Logical OR operator. It combines each element of the first vector with the corresponding element of the second vector and gives a output TRUE if one the elements is TRUE.	```\nv <-\nc(3,0,TRUE,2+2i)\nt <-\nc(4,0,FALSE,2+3i)\nprint(v|t)\n``` it produces the following result – [1] TRUE FALSE TRUE TRUE

| ! | It is called Logical NOT operator. Takes each element of the vector and gives the opposite logical value. | `v <-`
`c(3,0,TRUE,2+2i)`
`print(!v)`

it produces the following result –

`[1] FALSE TRUE FALSE FALSE` |

The logical operator && and || considers only the first element of the vectors and give a vector of single element as output.

Operator	Description	Example

&&	Called Logical AND operator. Takes first element of both the vectors and gives the TRUE only if both are TRUE.	`v <-`
		`c(3,0,TRUE,2+2i)`
		`t <-`
		`c(1,3,TRUE,2+3i)`
		`print(v&&t)`
		
		it produces the following result –
		
		`[1] TRUE`

||	Called Logical OR operator. Takes first element of both the vectors and gives the	`v <-`
		`c(0,0,TRUE,2+2i)`
		`t <-`
		`c(0,3,TRUE,2+3i)`
		`print(v||t)`

	TRUE if one of them is TRUE.	it produces the following result – [1] FALSE

Assignment Operators:

These operators are used to assign values to vectors.

Operator	Description	Example
<- or = or <<-	Called Left Assignment	v1 <- c(3,1,TRUE,2+3i) v2 <<- c(3,1,TRUE,2+3i) v3 = c(3,1,TRUE,2+3i) print(v1) print(v2) print(v3) it produces the following result – [1] 3+0i 1+0i 1+0i 2+3i [1] 3+0i 1+0i 1+0i 2+3i [1] 3+0i 1+0i 1+0i 2+3i
-> or ->>	Called Right Assignment	c(3,1,TRUE,2+3i) -> v1 c(3,1,TRUE,2+3i) ->> v2 print(v1) print(v2) it produces the

		following result –
		[1] 3+0i 1+0i 1+0i 2+3i [1] 3+0i 1+0i 1+0i 2+3i

Miscellaneous Operators:

These operators are used to for specific purpose and not general mathematical or logical computation.

Operator	Description	Example
:	Colon operator. It creates the series of numbers in sequence for a vector.	v <- 2:8 print(v) it produces the following result – [1] 2 3 4 5 6 7 8
%in%	This operator is used to identify if an element belongs to a	v1 <- 8 v2 <- 12 t <- 1:10 print(v1 %in% t) print(v2 %in% t) it produces the following result

	vector.	–
		[1] TRUE [1] FALSE
%*%	This operator is used to multiply a matrix with its transpose.	M = matrix(c(2,6,5,1,10,4), nrow = 2,ncol = 3,byrow = TRUE) t = M %*% t(M) print(t)
		it produces the following result –
		[,1] [,2] [1,] 65 82 [2,] 82 117

R - Decision making

Decision making structures require the programmer to specify one or more conditions to be evaluated or tested by the program, along with a statement or statements to be executed if the condition is determined to be **true**, and optionally, other statements to be executed if the condition is determined to be **false**.

Following is the general form of a typical decision making structure found in most of the programming languages −

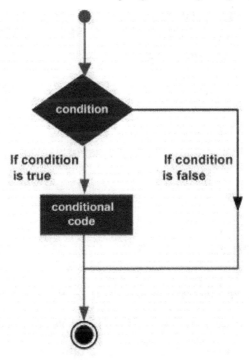

R provides the following types of decision making statements. Click the following links to check their detail.

Sr.No.	Statement & Description
1	if statement
	An **if** statement consists of a Boolean expression followed by one or more statements.
2	if...else statement
	An **if** statement can be followed by an optional **else** statement, which executes when the Boolean expression is false.
3	switch statement
	A **switch** statement allows a variable to be tested for equality against a list of values.

If Statement:

If statements can be very useful in R, as they are in any programming language,. Often, you want to make choices and take action dependent on a certain value.

Defining a choice in your code is pretty simple: If this condition is true, then carry out a certain task. Many programming languages let you do that with exactly those words: if . . . then. R makes it even easier: You can drop the word then and specify your choice in an ifstatement.

Syntax:

The basic syntax for creating an **if** statement in R is −

```
if(boolean_expression) {
   // statement(s) will execute if the boolean expression is
true.
}
```

If the Boolean expression evaluates to be **true**, then the block of code inside the if statement will be executed. If Boolean expression evaluates to be **false**, then the first set of code after the end of the if statement (after the closing curly brace) will be executed.

Flow Diagram:

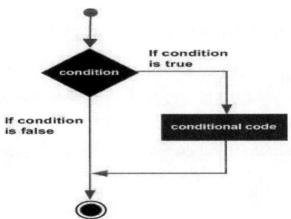

Example:

```
x <- 30L
if(is.integer(x)) {
  print("X is an Integer")
}
```

When the above code is compiled and executed, it produces the following result –

```
[1] "X is an Integer"
```

If...Else Statement:

An **if** statement can be followed by an optional **else** statement which executes when the boolean expression is false.

Syntax:

The basic syntax for creating an **if...else** statement in R is –

```
if(boolean_expression) {
  // statement(s) will execute if the boolean expression is true.
} else {
  // statement(s) will execute if the boolean expression is false.
}
```

If the Boolean expression evaluates to be **true**, then the **if block** of code will be executed, otherwise **else block** of code will be executed.

Flow Diagram

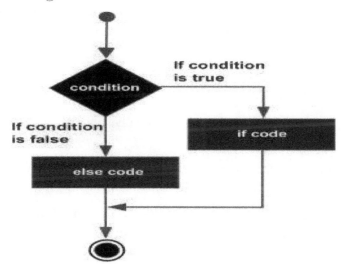

Example

```
x <- c("what","is","truth")

if("Truth" %in% x) {
   print("Truth is found")
} else {
   print("Truth is not found")
}
```

When the above code is compiled and executed, it produces the following result −

[1] "Truth is not found"

Here "Truth" and "truth" are two different strings.

The if...else if...else Statement:

An **if** statement can be followed by an optional **else if...else** statement, which is very useful to test various conditions using single if...else if statement.

When using **if, else if, else** statements there are few points to keep in mind.

- An **if** can have zero or one **else** and it must come after any **else if**'s.

- An **if** can have zero to many **else if**'s and they must come before the else.

- Once an **else if** succeeds, none of the remaining **else if**'s or **else**'s will be tested.

Syntax:

The basic syntax for creating an **if...else if...else** statement in R is −

```
if(boolean_expression 1) {
   // Executes when the boolean expression 1 is true.
} else if( boolean_expression 2) {
   // Executes when the boolean expression 2 is true.
} else if( boolean_expression 3) {
   // Executes when the boolean expression 3 is true.
} else {
   // executes when none of the above condition is true.
}
```

Example

```
x <- c("what","is","truth")

if("Truth" %in% x) {
  print("Truth is found the first time")
} else if ("truth" %in% x) {
  print("truth is found the second time")
} else {
  print("No truth found")
}
```

When the above code is compiled and executed, it produces the following result −

```
[1] "truth is found the second time"
```

Switch statement:

A **switch** statement allows a variable to be tested for equality against a list of values. Each value is called a case, and the variable being switched on is checked for each case.

Syntax:

The basic syntax for creating a switch statement in R is −

```
switch(expression, case1, case2, case3....)
```

The following rules apply to a switch statement −

- If the value of expression is not a character string it is coerced to integer.

- You can have any number of case statements within a switch. Each case is followed by the value to be compared to and a colon.

- If the value of the integer is between 1 and nargs()−1 (The max number of arguments)then the corresponding element of case condition is evaluated and the result returned.

- If expression evaluates to a character string then that string is matched (exactly) to the names of the elements.

- If there is more than one match, the first matching element is returned.

- No Default argument is available.

- In the case of no match, if there is a unnamed element of ... its value is returned. (If there is more than one such argument an error is returned.)

Flow Diagram:

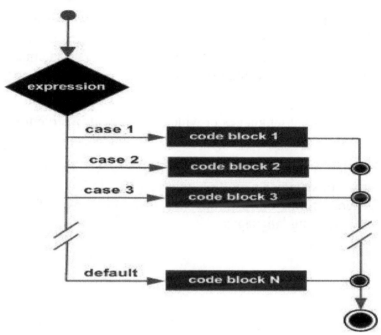

Example

```
x <- switch(
  3,
  "first",
  "second",
  "third",
  "fourth"
)
print(x)
```

When the above code is compiled and executed, it produces the following result –

```
[1] "third"
```

R - Loops

There may be a situation when you need to execute a block of code several number of times. In general, statements are executed sequentially. The first statement in a function is executed first, followed by the second, and so on.

Programming languages provide various control structures that allow for more complicated execution paths.

A loop statement allows us to execute a statement or group of statements multiple times and the following is the general form of a loop statement in most of the programming languages –

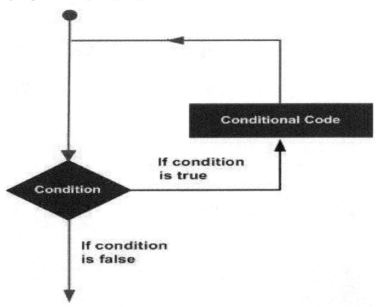

R programming language provides the following kinds of loop to handle looping requirements. Click the following links to check their detail.

Sr.No.	Loop Type & Description
1	repeat loop Executes a sequence of statements multiple times and abbreviates the code that manages the loop variable.
2	while loop Repeats a statement or group of statements while a given condition is true. It tests the condition before executing the loop body.
3	for loop Like a while statement, except that it tests the condition at the end of the loop body.

Repeat loop:

The **Repeat loop** executes the same code again and again until a stop condition is met.

Syntax:

The basic syntax for creating a repeat loop in R is −

```
repeat {
```

```
commands
if(condition) {
   break
}
}
```

Flow Diagram:

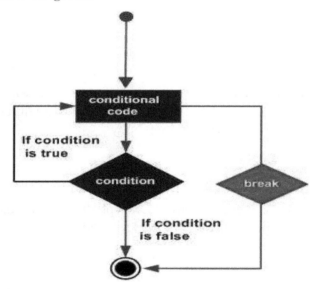

Example:

```
v <- c("Hello","loop")
cnt <- 2

repeat {
  print(v)
  cnt <- cnt+1

  if(cnt > 5) {
```

```
    break
    }
}
```

When the above code is compiled and executed, it produces the following result –

```
[1] "Hello" "loop"
[1] "Hello" "loop"
[1] "Hello" "loop"
[1] "Hello" "loop"
```

While loop:

The While loop executes the same code again and again until a stop condition is met.

Syntax:

The basic syntax for creating a while loop in R is –

```
while (test_expression) {
    statement
}
```

Flow Diagram:

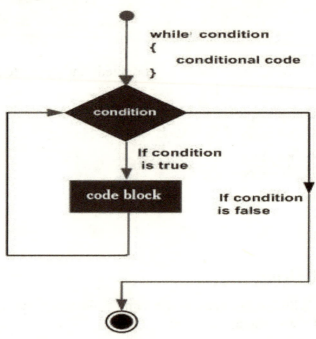

Here key point of the **while** loop is that the loop might not ever run. When the condition is tested and the result is false, the loop body will be skipped and the first statement after the while loop will be executed.

Example:

```
v <- c("Hello","while loop")
cnt <- 2

while (cnt < 7) {
  print(v)
  cnt = cnt + 1
}
```

When the above code is compiled and executed, it produces the following result –

```
[1] "Hello" "while loop"
[1] "Hello" "while loop"
[1] "Hello" "while loop"
[1] "Hello" "while loop"
[1] "Hello" "while loop"
```

Loop Control Statements:

Loop control statements change execution from its normal sequence. When execution leaves a scope, all automatic objects that were created in that scope are destroyed.

R supports the following control statements. Click the following links to check their detail.

Sr.No.	Control Statement & Description
1	break statement Terminates the **loop** statement and transfers execution to the statement immediately following the loop.
2	Next statement The **next** statement simulates the behavior of R switch.

Break statement:

The break statement in R programming language has the following two usages –

- When the break statement is encountered inside a loop, the loop is immediately terminated and program control resumes at the next statement following the loop.

- It can be used to terminate a case in the switch statement (covered in the next chapter).

Syntax

The basic syntax for creating a break statement in R is –

```
break
```

Flow Diagram:

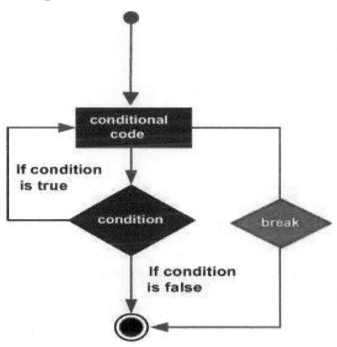

Example:

```
v <- c("Hello","loop")
cnt <- 2
```

```
repeat {
  print(v)
  cnt <- cnt + 1

  if(cnt > 5) {
    break
  }
}
```

When the above code is compiled and executed, it produces the following result –

```
[1] "Hello" "loop"
[1] "Hello" "loop"
[1] "Hello" "loop"
[1] "Hello" "loop"
```

Next statement:

The **next** statement in R programming language is useful when we want to skip the current iteration of a loop without terminating it. On encountering next, the R parser skips further evaluation and starts next iteration of the loop.

Syntax

The basic syntax for creating a next statement in R is –

```
next
```

Flow Diagram:

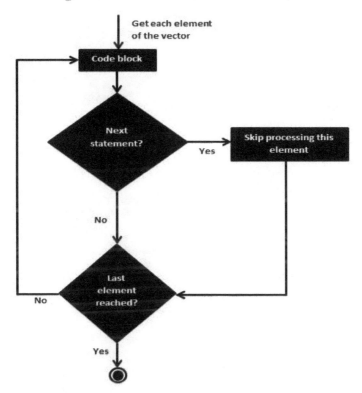

Example:

```
v <- LETTERS[1:6]
for ( i in v) {

  if (i == "D") {
    next
  }
  print(i)
}
```

When the above code is compiled and executed, it produces the following result –

```
[1] "A"
[1] "B"
[1] "C"
[1] "E"
[1] "F"
```

R - Functions

A function is a set of statements organized together to perform a specific task. R has a large number of in-built functions and the user can create their own functions.

In R, a function is an object so the R interpreter is able to pass control to the function, along with arguments that may be necessary for the function to accomplish the actions.

The function in turn performs its task and returns control to the interpreter as well as any result which may be stored in other objects.

Function Definition:

An R function is created by using the keyword **function**. The basic syntax of an R function definition is as follows –

```
function_name <- function(arg_1, arg_2, ...) {
   Function body
}
```

Function Components:

The different parts of a function are –

- **Function Name** – This is the actual name of the function. It is stored in R environment as an object with this name.

- **Arguments** – An argument is a placeholder. When a function is invoked, you pass a value to the argument. Arguments are optional; that is, a function may contain no arguments. Also arguments can have default values.

- **Function Body** – The function body contains a collection of statements that defines what the function does.

- **Return Value** – The return value of a function is the last expression in the function body to be evaluated.

R has many **in-built** functions which can be directly called in the program without defining them first. We can also create and use our own functions referred as **user defined** functions.

Built-in Function:

Simple examples of in-built functions are **seq()**, **mean()**, **max()**, **sum(x)** and **paste(...)**etc. They are directly called by user written programs. You can refer most widely used R functions.

```
# Create a sequence of numbers from 32 to 44.
print(seq(32,44))

# Find mean of numbers from 25 to 82.
print(mean(25:82))

# Find sum of numbers frm 41 to 68.
print(sum(41:68))
```

When we execute the above code, it produces the following result –

```
[1] 32 33 34 35 36 37 38 39 40 41 42 43 44
[1] 53.5
[1] 1526
```

User-defined Function:

We can create user-defined functions in R. They are specific to what a user wants and once created they can be used like the built-in functions. Below is an example of how a function is created and used.

```
# Create a function to print squares of numbers in
sequence.
new.function <- function(a) {
  for(i in 1:a) {
    b <- i^2
    print(b)
  }
}
```

Calling a Function:

```
# Create a function to print squares of numbers in
sequence.
new.function <- function(a) {
  for(i in 1:a) {
    b <- i^2
    print(b)
  }
```

```
}

# Call the function new.function supplying 6 as an
argument.
new.function(6)
```

When we execute the above code, it produces the following result −

```
[1] 1
[1] 4
[1] 9
[1] 16
[1] 25
[1] 36
```

Calling a Function without an Argument:

```
# Create a function without an argument.
new.function <- function() {
  for(i in 1:5) {
    print(i^2)
  }
}

# Call the function without supplying an argument.
new.function()
```

When we execute the above code, it produces the following result −

```
[1] 1
[1] 4
[1] 9
[1] 16
[1] 25
```

Calling a Function with Argument Values (by position and by name)

The arguments to a function call can be supplied in the same sequence as defined in the function or they can be supplied in a different sequence but assigned to the names of the arguments.

```
# Create a function with arguments.
new.function <- function(a,b,c) {
   result <- a * b + c
   print(result)
}

# Call the function by position of arguments.
new.function(5,3,11)

# Call the function by names of the arguments.
new.function(a = 11, b = 5, c = 3)
```

When we execute the above code, it produces the following result −

```
[1] 26
[1] 58
```

Calling a Function with Default Argument

We can define the value of the arguments in the function definition and call the function without supplying any argument to get the default result. But we can also call such functions by supplying new values of the argument and get non default result.

```
# Create a function with arguments.
new.function <- function(a = 3, b = 6) {
  result <- a * b
  print(result)
}

# Call the function without giving any argument.
new.function()

# Call the function with giving new values of the argument.
new.function(9,5)
```

When we execute the above code, it produces the following result –

```
[1] 18
[1] 45
```

Lazy Evaluation of Function

Arguments to functions are evaluated lazily, which means so they are evaluated only when needed by the function body.

```
# Create a function with arguments.
new.function <- function(a, b) {
  print(a^2)
  print(a)
  print(b)
}

# Evaluate the function without supplying one of the
arguments.
new.function(6)
```

When we execute the above code, it produces the
following result −

```
[1] 36
[1] 6
Error in print(b) : argument "b" is missing, with no default
```

R - Strings

Any value written within a pair of single quote or double quotes in R is treated as a string. Internally R stores every string within double quotes, even when you create them with single quote.

Rules Applied in String Construction:

- The quotes at the beginning and end of a string should be both double quotes or both single quote. They can not be mixed.

- Double quotes can be inserted into a string starting and ending with single quote.

- Single quote can be inserted into a string starting and ending with double quotes.

- Double quotes can not be inserted into a string starting and ending with double quotes.

- Single quote can not be inserted into a string starting and ending with single quote.

Examples of Valid Strings:

Following examples clarify the rules about creating a string in R.

```
a <- 'Start and end with single quote'
print(a)

b <- "Start and end with double quotes"
print(b)
```

R – A Beginner's Guide | 75

```r
c <- "single quote ' in between double quotes"
print(c)

d <- 'Double quotes " in between single quote'
print(d)
```

When the above code is run we get the following output –

```
[1] "Start and end with single quote"
[1] "Start and end with double quotes"
[1] "single quote ' in between double quote"
[1] "Double quote \" in between single quote"
```

Examples of Invalid Strings:

```r
e <- 'Mixed quotes"
print(e)

f <- 'Single quote ' inside single quote'
print(f)

g <- "Double quotes " inside double quotes"
print(g)
```

When we run the script it fails giving below results.

```
Error: unexpected symbol in:
"print(e)
f <- 'Single"
Execution halted
```

String Manipulation:

Concatenating Strings - paste() function:

Many strings in R are combined using the **paste()** function. It can take any number of arguments to be combined together.

Syntax:

The basic syntax for paste function is –

```
paste(..., sep = " ", collapse = NULL)
```

Following is the description of the parameters used –

- **...** represents any number of arguments to be combined.

- **sep** represents any separator between the arguments. It is optional.

- **collapse** is used to eliminate the space in between two strings. But not the space within two words of one string.

Example:

```
a <- "Hello"
b <- 'How'
c <- "are you? "

print(paste(a,b,c))

print(paste(a,b,c, sep = "-"))
```

```
print(paste(a,b,c, sep = "", collapse = ""))
```

When we execute the above code, it produces the following result −

```
[1] "Hello How are you? "
[1] "Hello-How-are you? "
[1] "HelloHoware you? "
```

Formatting numbers & strings - format() function

Numbers and strings can be formatted to a specific style using **format()** function.

Syntax:

The basic syntax for format function is −

```
format(x, digits, nsmall, scientific, width, justify = c("left", "right", "centre", "none"))
```

Following is the description of the parameters used −

- **x** is the vector input.

- **digits** is the total number of digits displayed.

- **nsmall** is the minimum number of digits to the right of the decimal point.

- **scientific** is set to TRUE to display scientific notation.

- **width** indicates the minimum width to be displayed by padding blanks in the beginning.

- **justify** is the display of the string to left, right or center.

Example:

```
# Total number of digits displayed. Last digit rounded off.
result <- format(23.123456789, digits = 9)
print(result)

# Display numbers in scientific notation.
result <- format(c(6, 13.14521), scientific = TRUE)
print(result)

# The minimum number of digits to the right of the decimal
point.
result <- format(23.47, nsmall = 5)
print(result)

# Format treats everything as a string.
result <- format(6)
print(result)

# Numbers are padded with blank in the beginning for
width.
result <- format(13.7, width = 6)
print(result)

# Left justify strings.
result <- format("Hello", width = 8, justify = "l")
print(result)

# Justfy string with center.
result <- format("Hello", width = 8, justify = "c")
print(result)
```

When we execute the above code, it produces the following result –

```
[1] "23.1234568"
[1] "6.000000e+00" "1.314521e+01"
[1] "23.47000"
[1] "6"
[1] "  13.7"
[1] "Hello  "
[1] " Hello  "
```

Counting number of characters in a string - nchar() function:

This function counts the number of characters including spaces in a string.

Syntax:

The basic syntax for nchar() function is –

```
nchar(x)
```

Following is the description of the parameters used –

- **x** is the vector input.

Example:

```
result <- nchar("Count the number of characters")
print(result)
```

When we execute the above code, it produces the following result –

```
[1] 30
```

Changing the case - toupper() & tolower() functions

These functions change the case of characters of a string.

Syntax:

The basic syntax for toupper() & tolower() function is –

```
toupper(x)
tolower(x)
```

Following is the description of the parameters used –

- **x** is the vector input.

Example:

```
# Changing to Upper case.
result <- toupper("Changing To Upper")
print(result)

# Changing to lower case.
result <- tolower("Changing To Lower")
print(result)
```

When we execute the above code, it produces the following result –

```
[1] "CHANGING TO UPPER"
[1] "changing to lower"
```

Extracting parts of a string - substring() function:

This function extracts parts of a String.

Syntax:

The basic syntax for substring() function is −

```
substring(x,first,last)
```

Following is the description of the parameters used −

- **x** is the character vector input.

- **first** is the position of the first character to be extracted.

- **last** is the position of the last character to be extracted.

Example:

```
# Extract characters from 5th to 7th position.
result <- substring("Extract", 5, 7)
print(result)
```

When we execute the above code, it produces the following result −

```
[1] "act"
```

R - Vectors

Vectors are the most basic R data objects and there are six types of atomic vectors. They are logical, integer, double, complex, character and raw.

Vector Creation

Single Element Vector:

Even when you write just one value in R, it becomes a vector of length 1 and belongs to one of the above vector types.

```
# Atomic vector of type character.
print("abc");

# Atomic vector of type double.
print(12.5)

# Atomic vector of type integer.
print(63L)

# Atomic vector of type logical.
print(TRUE)

# Atomic vector of type complex.
print(2+3i)

# Atomic vector of type raw.
print(charToRaw('hello'))
```

When we execute the above code, it produces the following result −

```
[1] "abc"
[1] 12.5
[1] 63
[1] TRUE
[1] 2+3i
[1] 68 65 6c 6c 6f
```

Multiple Elements Vector:

Using colon operator with numeric data

```
# Creating a sequence from 5 to 13.
v <- 5:13
print(v)

# Creating a sequence from 6.6 to 12.6.
v <- 6.6:12.6
print(v)

# If the final element specified does not belong to the
sequence then it is discarded.
v <- 3.8:11.4
print(v)
```

When we execute the above code, it produces the following result −

```
[1] 5 6 7 8 9 10 11 12 13
[1] 6.6 7.6 8.6 9.6 10.6 11.6 12.6
[1] 3.8 4.8 5.8 6.8 7.8 8.8 9.8 10.8
```

Using sequence (Seq.) operator

```
# Create vector with elements from 5 to 9 incrementing by
0.4.
print(seq(5, 9, by = 0.4))
```

When we execute the above code, it produces the following result −

```
[1] 5.0 5.4 5.8 6.2 6.6 7.0 7.4 7.8 8.2 8.6 9.0
```

Using the c() function:

The non-character values are coerced to character type if one of the elements is a character.

```
# The logical and numeric values are converted to
characters.
s <- c('apple','red',5,TRUE)
print(s)
```

When we execute the above code, it produces the following result −

```
[1] "apple" "red" "5"    "TRUE"
```

Accessing Vector Elements:

Elements of a Vector are accessed using indexing. The [ ] **brackets** are used for indexing. Indexing starts with position 1. Giving a negative value in the index drops that element from result.**TRUE, FALSE** or **0** and **1** can also be used for indexing.

```
# Accessing vector elements using position.
t <- c("Sun","Mon","Tue","Wed","Thurs","Fri","Sat")
u <- t[c(2,3,6)]
print(u)

# Accessing vector elements using logical indexing.
v                                                     <-
t[c(TRUE,FALSE,FALSE,FALSE,FALSE,TRUE,FALSE)
]
print(v)

# Accessing vector elements using negative indexing.
x <- t[c(-2,-5)]
print(x)

# Accessing vector elements using 0/1 indexing.
y <- t[c(0,0,0,0,0,0,1)]
print(y)
```

When we execute the above code, it produces the following result –

```
[1] "Mon" "Tue" "Fri"
[1] "Sun" "Fri"
[1] "Sun" "Tue" "Wed" "Fri" "Sat"
[1] "Sun"
```

Vector Manipulation:

Vector arithmetic:

Two vectors of same length can be added, subtracted, multiplied or divided giving the result as a vector output.

```
# Create two vectors.
v1 <- c(3,8,4,5,0,11)
v2 <- c(4,11,0,8,1,2)

# Vector addition.
add.result <- v1+v2
print(add.result)

# Vector subtraction.
sub.result <- v1-v2
print(sub.result)

# Vector multiplication.
multi.result <- v1*v2
print(multi.result)

# Vector division.
divi.result <- v1/v2
print(divi.result)
```

When we execute the above code, it produces the following result –

```
[1]  7 19  4 13  1 13
[1] -1 -3  4 -3 -1  9
[1] 12 88  0 40  0 22
[1] 0.7500000 0.7272727       Inf 0.6250000 0.0000000
5.5000000
```

Vector Element Recycling:

If we apply arithmetic operations to two vectors of unequal length, then the elements of the shorter vector are recycled to complete the operations.

```
v1 <- c(3,8,4,5,0,11)
v2 <- c(4,11)
# V2 becomes c(4,11,4,11,4,11)

add.result <- v1+v2
print(add.result)

sub.result <- v1-v2
print(sub.result)
```

When we execute the above code, it produces the following result –

```
[1]  7 19  8 16  4 22
[1] -1 -3  0 -6 -4  0
```

Vector Element Sorting

Elements in a vector can be sorted using the **sort()** function.

```
v <- c(3,8,4,5,0,11, -9, 304)

# Sort the elements of the vector.
sort.result <- sort(v)
print(sort.result)

# Sort the elements in the reverse order.
revsort.result <- sort(v, decreasing = TRUE)
print(revsort.result)

# Sorting character vectors.
v <- c("Red","Blue","yellow","violet")
sort.result <- sort(v)
print(sort.result)
```

```
# Sorting character vectors in reverse order.
revsort.result <- sort(v, decreasing = TRUE)
print(revsort.result)
```

When we execute the above code, it produces the following result −

```
[1] -9  0  3  4  5  8 11 304
[1] 304 11  8  5  4  3  0 -9
[1] "Blue" "Red"   "violet" "yellow"
[1] "yellow" "violet" "Red"   "Blue"
```

R - Lists

Lists are the R objects which contain elements of different types like – numbers, strings, vectors and another list inside it. A list can also contain a matrix or a function as its elements. List is created using **list()** function.

Creating a List:

Following is an example to create a list containing strings, numbers, vectors and a logical values.

```
# Create a list containing strings, numbers, vectors and a
logical
# values.
list_data <- list("Red", "Green", c(21,32,11), TRUE, 51.23,
119.1)
print(list_data)
```

When we execute the above code, it produces the following result –

```
[[1]]
[1] "Red"

[[2]]
[1] "Green"

[[3]]
[1] 21 32 11

[[4]]
[1] TRUE
```

```
[[5]]
[1] 51.23

[[6]]
[1] 119.1
```

Naming List Elements:

The list elements can be given names and they can be accessed using these names.

```
# Create a list containing a vector, a matrix and a list.
list_data <- list(c("Jan","Feb","Mar"), matrix(c(3,9,5,1,-2,8), nrow = 2),
  list("green",12.3))

# Give names to the elements in the list.
names(list_data) <- c("1st Quarter", "A_Matrix", "A Inner list")

# Show the list.
print(list_data)
```

When we execute the above code, it produces the following result −

```
$`1st_Quarter`
[1] "Jan" "Feb" "Mar"

$A_Matrix
     [,1] [,2] [,3]
[1,]   3    5   -2
[2,]   9    1    8
```

```
$A_Inner_list
$A_Inner_list[[1]]
[1] "green"

$A_Inner_list[[2]]
[1] 12.3
```

Accessing List Elements:

Elements of the list can be accessed by the index of the element in the list. In case of named lists it can also be accessed using the names.

We continue to use the list in the above example –

```
# Create a list containing a vector, a matrix and a list.
list_data <- list(c("Jan","Feb","Mar"), matrix(c(3,9,5,1,-2,8), nrow = 2),
   list("green",12.3))

# Give names to the elements in the list.
names(list_data) <- c("1st Quarter", "A_Matrix", "A Inner list")

# Access the first element of the list.
print(list_data[1])

# Access the thrid element. As it is also a list, all its elements will be printed.
print(list_data[3])

# Access the list element using the name of the element.
print(list_data$A_Matrix)
```

When we execute the above code, it produces the following result −

```
$`1st_Quarter`
[1] "Jan" "Feb" "Mar"

$A_Inner_list
$A_Inner_list[[1]]
[1] "green"

$A_Inner_list[[2]]
[1] 12.3


   [,1] [,2] [,3]
[1,]  3   5   -2
[2,]  9   1    8
```

Manipulating List Elements:

We can add, delete and update list elements as shown below. We can add and delete elements only at the end of a list. But we can update any element.

```
# Create a list containing a vector, a matrix and a list.
list_data  <-  list(c("Jan","Feb","Mar"),  matrix(c(3,9,5,1,-2,8), nrow = 2),
  list("green",12.3))

# Give names to the elements in the list.
names(list_data) <- c("1st Quarter", "A_Matrix", "A Inner list")

# Add element at the end of the list.
list_data[4] <- "New element"
print(list_data[4])
```

```
# Remove the last element.
list_data[4] <- NULL

# Print the 4th Element.
print(list_data[4])

# Update the 3rd Element.
list_data[3] <- "updated element"
print(list_data[3])
```

When we execute the above code, it produces the following result –

```
[[1]]
[1] "New element"

$<NA>
NULL

$`A Inner list`
[1] "updated element"
```

Merging Lists:

You can merge many lists into one list by placing all the lists inside one list() function.

```
# Create two lists.
list1 <- list(1,2,3)
list2 <- list("Sun","Mon","Tue")

# Merge the two lists.
merged.list <- c(list1,list2)
```

```
# Print the merged list.
print(merged.list)
```

When we execute the above code, it produces the following result −

```
[[1]]
[1] 1

[[2]]
[1] 2

[[3]]
[1] 3

[[4]]
[1] "Sun"

[[5]]
[1] "Mon"

[[6]]
[1] "Tue"
```

Converting List to Vector:

A list can be converted to a vector so that the elements of the vector can be used for further manipulation. All the arithmetic operations on vectors can be applied after the list is converted into vectors. To do this conversion, we use the **unlist()** function. It takes the list as input and produces a vector.

```
# Create lists.
list1 <- list(1:5)
print(list1)

list2 <-list(10:14)
print(list2)

# Convert the lists to vectors.
v1 <- unlist(list1)
v2 <- unlist(list2)

print(v1)
print(v2)

# Now add the vectors
result <- v1+v2
print(result)
```

When we execute the above code, it produces the following result −

```
[[1]]
[1] 1 2 3 4 5

[[1]]
[1] 10 11 12 13 14

[1] 1 2 3 4 5
[1] 10 11 12 13 14
[1] 11 13 15 17 19
```

R - Matrices

Matrices are the R objects in which the elements are arranged in a two-dimensional rectangular layout. They contain elements of the same atomic types. Though we can create a matrix containing only characters or only logical values, they are not of much use. We use matrices containing numeric elements to be used in mathematical calculations.

A Matrix is created using the **matrix()** function.

Syntax:

The basic syntax for creating a matrix in R is −

matrix(data, nrow, ncol, byrow, dimnames)

Following is the description of the parameters used −

- **data** is the input vector which becomes the data elements of the matrix.

- **nrow** is the number of rows to be created.

- **ncol** is the number of columns to be created.

- **byrow** is a logical clue. If TRUE then the input vector elements are arranged by row.

- **dimname** is the names assigned to the rows and columns.

Example:

Create a matrix taking a vector of numbers as input.

```
# Elements are arranged sequentially by row.
M <- matrix(c(3:14), nrow = 4, byrow = TRUE)
print(M)

# Elements are arranged sequentially by column.
N <- matrix(c(3:14), nrow = 4, byrow = FALSE)
print(N)

# Define the column and row names.
rownames = c("row1", "row2", "row3", "row4")
colnames = c("col1", "col2", "col3")

P <- matrix(c(3:14), nrow = 4, byrow = TRUE, dimnames
= list(rownames, colnames))
print(P)
```

When we execute the above code, it produces the following result −

```
     [,1] [,2] [,3]
[1,]   3    4    5
[2,]   6    7    8
[3,]   9   10   11
[4,]  12   13   14
     [,1] [,2] [,3]
[1,]   3    7   11
[2,]   4    8   12
[3,]   5    9   13
[4,]   6   10   14
     col1 col2 col3
row1   3    4    5
row2   6    7    8
row3   9   10   11
row4  12   13   14
```

Accessing Elements of a Matrix:

Elements of a matrix can be accessed by using the column and row index of the element. We consider the matrix P above to find the specific elements below.

```
# Define the column and row names.
rownames = c("row1", "row2", "row3", "row4")
colnames = c("col1", "col2", "col3")

# Create the matrix.
P <- matrix(c(3:14), nrow = 4, byrow = TRUE, dimnames
= list(rownames, colnames))

# Access the element at 3rd column and 1st row.
print(P[1,3])

# Access the element at 2nd column and 4th row.
print(P[4,2])

# Access only the 2nd row.
print(P[2,])

# Access only the 3rd column.
print(P[,3])
```

When we execute the above code, it produces the following result –

```
[1] 5
[1] 13
col1 col2 col3
  6   7   8
row1 row2 row3 row4
  5   8  11  14
```

Matrix Computations:

Various mathematical operations are performed on the matrices using the R operators. The result of the operation is also a matrix.

The dimensions (number of rows and columns) should be same for the matrices involved in the operation.

Matrix Addition & Subtraction

```
# Create two 2x3 matrices.
matrix1 <- matrix(c(3, 9, -1, 4, 2, 6), nrow = 2)
print(matrix1)

matrix2 <- matrix(c(5, 2, 0, 9, 3, 4), nrow = 2)
print(matrix2)

# Add the matrices.
result <- matrix1 + matrix2
cat("Result of addition","\n")
print(result)

# Subtract the matrices
result <- matrix1 - matrix2
cat("Result of subtraction","\n")
print(result)
```

When we execute the above code, it produces the following result −

```
     [,1] [,2] [,3]
[1,]   3   -1   2
[2,]   9    4   6
```

```
     [,1] [,2] [,3]
[1,]   5   0   3
[2,]   2   9   4
Result of addition
     [,1] [,2] [,3]
[1,]   8  -1   5
[2,]  11  13  10
Result of subtraction
     [,1] [,2] [,3]
[1,]  -2  -1  -1
[2,]   7  -5   2
```

Matrix Multiplication & Division:

```
# Create two 2x3 matrices.
matrix1 <- matrix(c(3, 9, -1, 4, 2, 6), nrow = 2)
print(matrix1)

matrix2 <- matrix(c(5, 2, 0, 9, 3, 4), nrow = 2)
print(matrix2)

# Multiply the matrices.
result <- matrix1 * matrix2
cat("Result of multiplication","\n")
print(result)

# Divide the matrices
result <- matrix1 / matrix2
cat("Result of division","\n")
print(result)
```

When we execute the above code, it produces the following result −

```
     [,1] [,2] [,3]
[1,]   3  -1   2
[2,]   9   4   6
     [,1] [,2] [,3]
[1,]   5   0   3
[2,]   2   9   4
Result of multiplication
     [,1] [,2] [,3]
[1,]  15   0   6
[2,]  18  36  24
Result of division
     [,1]    [,2]     [,3]
[1,] 0.6    -Inf 0.6666667
[2,] 4.5 0.4444444 1.5000000
```

R - Arrays

Arrays are the R data objects which can store data in more than two dimensions. For example − If we create an array of dimension (2, 3, 4) then it creates 4 rectangular matrices each with 2 rows and 3 columns. Arrays can store only data type.

An array is created using the **array()** function. It takes vectors as input and uses the values in the **dim** parameter to create an array.

Example:

The following example creates an array of two 3x3 matrices each with 3 rows and 3 columns.

```
# Create two vectors of different lengths.
vector1 <- c(5,9,3)
vector2 <- c(10,11,12,13,14,15)

# Take these vectors as input to the array.
result <- array(c(vector1,vector2),dim = c(3,3,2))
print(result)
```

When we execute the above code, it produces the following result −

```
, , 1

     [,1] [,2] [,3]
[1,]   5   10   13
[2,]   9   11   14
[3,]   3   12   15
```

```
, , 2

     [,1] [,2] [,3]
[1,]   5  10   13
[2,]   9  11   14
[3,]   3  12   15
```

Naming Columns and Rows:

We can give names to the rows, columns and matrices in the array by using the **dimnames** parameter.

```
# Create two vectors of different lengths.
vector1 <- c(5,9,3)
vector2 <- c(10,11,12,13,14,15)
column.names <- c("COL1","COL2","COL3")
row.names <- c("ROW1","ROW2","ROW3")
matrix.names <- c("Matrix1","Matrix2")

# Take these vectors as input to the array.
result <- array(c(vector1,vector2),dim = c(3,3,2),dimnames
= list(row.names,column.names,
   matrix.names))
print(result)
```

When we execute the above code, it produces the following result –

```
, , Matrix1

     COL1 COL2 COL3
ROW1   5   10   13
ROW2   9   11   14
ROW3   3   12   15
```

```
, , Matrix2

   COL1 COL2 COL3
ROW1  5  10  13
ROW2  9  11  14
ROW3  3  12  15
```

Accessing Array Elements:

```
# Create two vectors of different lengths.
vector1 <- c(5,9,3)
vector2 <- c(10,11,12,13,14,15)
column.names <- c("COL1","COL2","COL3")
row.names <- c("ROW1","ROW2","ROW3")
matrix.names <- c("Matrix1","Matrix2")

# Take these vectors as input to the array.
result <- array(c(vector1,vector2),dim = c(3,3,2),dimnames
= list(row.names,
  column.names, matrix.names))

# Print the third row of the second matrix of the array.
print(result[3,,2])

# Print the element in the 1st row and 3rd column of the 1st
matrix.
print(result[1,3,1])

# Print the 2nd Matrix.
print(result[,,2])
```

When we execute the above code, it produces the following result −

```
COL1 COL2 COL3
  3   12   15
[1] 13
    COL1 COL2 COL3
ROW1   5   10   13
ROW2   9   11   14
ROW3   3   12   15
```

Manipulating Array Elements:

As array is made up matrices in multiple dimensions, the operations on elements of array are carried out by accessing elements of the matrices.

```r
# Create two vectors of different lengths.
vector1 <- c(5,9,3)
vector2 <- c(10,11,12,13,14,15)

# Take these vectors as input to the array.
array1 <- array(c(vector1,vector2),dim = c(3,3,2))

# Create two vectors of different lengths.
vector3 <- c(9,1,0)
vector4 <- c(6,0,11,3,14,1,2,6,9)
array2 <- array(c(vector1,vector2),dim = c(3,3,2))

# create matrices from these arrays.
matrix1 <- array1[,,2]
matrix2 <- array2[,,2]

# Add the matrices.
result <- matrix1+matrix2
print(result)
```

When we execute the above code, it produces the following result −

```
     [,1] [,2] [,3]
[1,]  10   20   26
[2,]  18   22   28
[3,]   6   24   30
```

Calculations Across Array Elements

We can do calculations across the elements in an array using the **apply()** function.

Syntax:

apply(x, margin, fun)

Following is the description of the parameters used −

- **x** is an array.

- **margin** is the name of the data set used.

- **fun** is the function to be applied across the elements of the array.

Example:

We use the apply() function below to calculate the sum of the elements in the rows of an array across all the matrices.

```
# Create two vectors of different lengths.
vector1 <- c(5,9,3)
vector2 <- c(10,11,12,13,14,15)

# Take these vectors as input to the array.
```

```
new.array <- array(c(vector1,vector2),dim = c(3,3,2))
print(new.array)

# Use apply to calculate the sum of the rows across all the
matrices.
result <- apply(new.array, c(1), sum)
print(result)
```

When we execute the above code, it produces the following result −

```
, , 1

     [,1] [,2] [,3]
[1,]   5   10   13
[2,]   9   11   14
[3,]   3   12   15

, , 2

     [,1] [,2] [,3]
[1,]   5   10   13
[2,]   9   11   14
[3,]   3   12   15

[1] 56 68 60
```

R - Factors

Factors are the data objects which are used to categorize the data and store it as levels. They can store both strings and integers. They are useful in the columns which have a limited number of unique values. Like "Male, "Female" and True, False etc. They are useful in data analysis for statistical modeling.

Factors are created using the **factor ()** function by taking a vector as input.

Example:

```
# Create a vector as input.
data                                                    <-
c("East","West","East","North","North","East","West","We
st","West","East","North")

print(data)
print(is.factor(data))

# Apply the factor function.
factor_data <- factor(data)

print(factor_data)
print(is.factor(factor_data))
```

When we execute the above code, it produces the following result −

```
[1] "East" "West" "East" "North" "North" "East" "West"
"West" "West" "East" "North"
[1] FALSE
```

```
[1] East West East North North East West West West
East North
Levels: East North West
[1] TRUE
```

Factors in Data Frame

On creating any data frame with a column of text data, R treats the text column as categorical data and creates factors on it.

```
# Create the vectors for data frame.
height <- c(132,151,162,139,166,147,122)
weight <- c(48,49,66,53,67,52,40)
gender                                         <-
c("male","male","female","female","male","female","male")

# Create the data frame.
input_data <- data.frame(height,weight,gender)
print(input_data)

# Test if the gender column is a factor.
print(is.factor(input_data$gender))

# Print the gender column so see the levels.
print(input_data$gender)
```

When we execute the above code, it produces the following result −

```
  height weight gender
1   132    48   male
2   151    49   male
```

```
3   162   66 female
4   139   53 female
5   166   67  male
6   147   52 female
7   122   40  male
[1] TRUE
[1] male   male   female female male   female male
Levels: female male
```

Changing the Order of Levels:

The order of the levels in a factor can be changed by applying the factor function again with new order of the levels.

```
data                                              <-
c("East","West","East","North","North","East","West",
  "West","West","East","North")
# Create the factors
factor_data <- factor(data)
print(factor_data)

# Apply the factor function with required order of the level.
new_order_data      <-      factor(factor_data,levels    =
c("East","West","North"))
print(new_order_data)
```

When we execute the above code, it produces the following result −

```
[1] East  West  East  North North East  West  West  West
East  North
Levels: East North West
```

```
[1] East West East North North East West West West
East North
Levels: East West North
```

Generating Factor Levels:

We can generate factor levels by using the **gl()** function. It takes two integers as input which indicates how many levels and how many times each level.

Syntax:

gl(n, k, labels)

Following is the description of the parameters used −

- **n** is a integer giving the number of levels.

- **k** is a integer giving the number of replications.

- **labels** is a vector of labels for the resulting factor levels.

Example:

```
v <- gl(3, 4, labels = c("Tampa", "Seattle","Boston"))
print(v)
```

When we execute the above code, it produces the following result −

```
Tampa  Tampa  Tampa  Tampa  Seattle Seattle Seattle
Seattle Boston
[10] Boston  Boston  Boston
Levels: Tampa Seattle Boston
```

R - Data Frames

A data frame is a table or a two-dimensional array-like structure in which each column contains values of one variable and each row contains one set of values from each column.

Following are the characteristics of a data frame.

- The column names should be non-empty.
- The row names should be unique.
- The data stored in a data frame can be of numeric, factor or character type.
- Each column should contain same number of data items.

Create Data Frame:

```
# Create the data frame.
emp.data <- data.frame(
  emp_id = c (1:5),
  emp_name = c("Rick","Dan","Michelle","Ryan","Gary"),
  salary = c(623.3,515.2,611.0,729.0,843.25),

  start_date = as.Date(c("2012-01-01", "2013-09-23",
"2014-11-15", "2014-05-11",
    "2015-03-27")),
  stringsAsFactors = FALSE
)
# Print the data frame.
print(emp.data)
```

When we execute the above code, it produces the following result −

```
emp_id  emp_name   salary   start_date
1   1   Rick      623.30   2012-01-01
2   2   Dan       515.20   2013-09-23
3   3   Michelle  611.00   2014-11-15
4   4   Ryan      729.00   2014-05-11
5   5   Gary      843.25   2015-03-27
```

Get the Structure of the Data Frame

The structure of the data frame can be seen by using **str()** function.

```
# Create the data frame.
emp.data <- data.frame(
  emp_id = c (1:5),
  emp_name = c("Rick","Dan","Michelle","Ryan","Gary"),
  salary = c(623.3,515.2,611.0,729.0,843.25),

  start_date = as.Date(c("2012-01-01", "2013-09-23",
"2014-11-15", "2014-05-11",
    "2015-03-27")),
  stringsAsFactors = FALSE
)
# Get the structure of the data frame.
str(emp.data)
```

When we execute the above code, it produces the following result −

```
'data.frame':  5 obs. of  4 variables:
$ emp_id   : int 1 2 3 4 5
$ emp_name : chr "Rick" "Dan" "Michelle" "Ryan" ...
```

```
$ salary   : num  623 515 611 729 843
$ start_date: Date, format: "2012-01-01" "2013-09-23"
"2014-11-15" "2014-05-11" ...
```

Summary of Data in Data Frame

The statistical summary and nature of the data can be obtained by applying **summary()** function.

```
# Create the data frame.
emp.data <- data.frame(
   emp_id = c (1:5),
   emp_name = c("Rick","Dan","Michelle","Ryan","Gary"),
   salary = c(623.3,515.2,611.0,729.0,843.25),

   start_date   =   as.Date(c("2012-01-01",   "2013-09-23",
"2014-11-15","2014-05-11",
   "2015-03-27")),
   stringsAsFactors = FALSE
)
# Print the summary.
print(summary(emp.data))
```

When we execute the above code, it produces the following result −

```
   emp_id   emp_name        salary     start_date
Min.  :1  Length:5        Min.  :515.2  Min.  :2012-01-
01
1st Qu.:2  Class :character  1st Qu.:611.0  1st Qu.:2013-
09-23
Median :3  Mode :character   Median :623.3   Median
:2014-05-11
```

Mean :3	Mean :664.4	Mean :2014-01-14
3rd Qu.:4	3rd Qu.:729.0	3rd Qu.:2014-11-15
Max. :5	Max. :843.2	Max. :2015-03-27

Extract Data from Data Frame:

Extract specific column from a data frame using column name.

```
# Create the data frame.
emp.data <- data.frame(
  emp_id = c (1:5),
  emp_name = c("Rick","Dan","Michelle","Ryan","Gary"),
  salary = c(623.3,515.2,611.0,729.0,843.25),

  start_date = as.Date(c("2012-01-01","2013-09-23","2014-
11-15","2014-05-11",
    "2015-03-27")),
  stringsAsFactors = FALSE
)
# Extract Specific columns.
result <- data.frame(emp.data$emp_name,emp.data$salary)
print(result)
```

When we execute the above code, it produces the following result −

	emp.data.emp_name	emp.data.salary
1	Rick	623.30
2	Dan	515.20
3	Michelle	611.00
4	Ryan	729.00
5	Gary	843.25

Extract the first two rows and then all columns

```
# Create the data frame.
emp.data <- data.frame(
  emp_id = c (1:5),
  emp_name = c("Rick","Dan","Michelle","Ryan","Gary"),
  salary = c(623.3,515.2,611.0,729.0,843.25),

  start_date    =    as.Date(c("2012-01-01",    "2013-09-23",
"2014-11-15", "2014-05-11",
    "2015-03-27")),
  stringsAsFactors = FALSE
)
# Extract first two rows.
result <- emp.data[1:2,]
print(result)
```

When we execute the above code, it produces the
following result –

```
  emp_id  emp_name  salary  start_date
1    1      Rick     623.3   2012-01-01
2    2      Dan      515.2   2013-09-23
```

Extract 3rd and 5th row with 2nd and 4th column

```
# Create the data frame.
emp.data <- data.frame(
  emp_id = c (1:5),
  emp_name = c("Rick","Dan","Michelle","Ryan","Gary"),
  salary = c(623.3,515.2,611.0,729.0,843.25),

        start_date  =  as.Date(c("2012-01-01", "2013-09-
23", "2014-11-15", "2014-05-11",
```

```
   "2015-03-27")),
  stringsAsFactors = FALSE
)

# Extract 3rd and 5th row with 2nd and 4th column.
result <- emp.data[c(3,5),c(2,4)]
print(result)
```

When we execute the above code, it produces the following result −

```
  emp_name start_date
3 Michelle 2014-11-15
5    Gary 2015-03-27
```

Expand Data Frame

A data frame can be expanded by adding columns and rows.

Add Column

Just add the column vector using a new column name.

```
# Create the data frame.
emp.data <- data.frame(
  emp_id = c (1:5),
  emp_name = c("Rick","Dan","Michelle","Ryan","Gary"),
  salary = c(623.3,515.2,611.0,729.0,843.25),

  start_date   =   as.Date(c("2012-01-01", "2013-09-23",
"2014-11-15", "2014-05-11",
   "2015-03-27")),
  stringsAsFactors = FALSE
```

```
)
# Add the "dept" coulmn.
emp.data$dept                              <-
c("IT","Operations","IT","HR","Finance")
v <- emp.data
print(v)
```

When we execute the above code, it produces the following result –

emp_id	emp_name	salary	start_date	dept
1	1	Rick	623.30	2012-01-01	IT
2	2	Dan	515.20	2013-09-23	Operations
3	3	Michelle	611.00	2014-11-15	IT
4	4	Ryan	729.00	2014-05-11	HR
5	5	Gary	843.25	2015-03-27	Finance

Add Row

To add more rows permanently to an existing data frame, we need to bring in the new rows in the same structure as the existing data frame and use the **rbind()** function.

In the example below we create a data frame with new rows and merge it with the existing data frame to create the final data frame.

```
# Create the first data frame.
emp.data <- data.frame(
  emp_id = c (1:5),
  emp_name = c("Rick","Dan","Michelle","Ryan","Gary"),
  salary = c(623.3,515.2,611.0,729.0,843.25),
```

```
  start_date  =  as.Date(c("2012-01-01",  "2013-09-23",
"2014-11-15","2014-05-11",
   "2015-03-27")),
  dept = c("IT","Operations","IT","HR","Finance"),
  stringsAsFactors = FALSE
)

# Create the second data frame
emp.newdata <-    data.frame(
  emp_id = c (6:8),
  emp_name = c("Rasmi","Pranab","Tusar"),
  salary = c(578.0,722.5,632.8),
  start_date = as.Date(c("2013-05-21","2013-07-30","2014-
06-17")),
  dept = c("IT","Operations","Fianance"),
  stringsAsFactors = FALSE
)

# Bind the two data frames.
emp.finaldata <- rbind(emp.data,emp.newdata)
print(emp.finaldata)
```

When we execute the above code, it produces the following result –

	emp_id	emp_name	salary	start_date	dept
1	1	Rick	623.30	2012-01-01	IT
2	2	Dan	515.20	2013-09-23	Operations
3	3	Michelle	611.00	2014-11-15	IT
4	4	Ryan	729.00	2014-05-11	HR
5	5	Gary	843.25	2015-03-27	Finance
6	6	Rasmi	578.00	2013-05-21	IT
7	7	Pranab	722.50	2013-07-30	Operations
8	8	Tusar	632.80	2014-06-17	Fianance

R - Packages

R packages are a collection of R functions, complied code and sample data. They are stored under a directory called **"library"** in the R environment. By default, R installs a set of packages during installation. More packages are added later, when they are needed for some specific purpose. When we start the R console, only the default packages are available by default. Other packages which are already installed have to be loaded explicitly to be used by the R program that is going to use them.

All the packages available in R language are listed at R Packages.

Below is a list of commands to be used to check, verify and use the R packages.

Check Available R Packages:

Get library locations containing R packages

```
.libPaths()
```

When we execute the above code, it produces the following result. It may vary depending on the local settings of your pc.

```
[2] "C:/Program Files/R/R-3.2.2/library"
```

Get the list of all the packages installed:

```
library()
```

When we execute the above code, it produces the following result. It may vary depending on the local settings of your pc.

Packages in library 'C:/Program Files/R/R-3.2.2/library':

base	The R Base Package
boot	Bootstrap Functions (Originally by Angelo Canty
	for S)
class	Functions for Classification
cluster	"Finding Groups in Data": Cluster Analysis
	Extended Rousseeuw et al.
codetools	Code Analysis Tools for R
compiler	The R Compiler Package
datasets	The R Datasets Package
foreign	Read Data Stored by 'Minitab', 'S', 'SAS',
	'SPSS', 'Stata', 'Systat', 'Weka', 'dBase', ...
graphics	The R Graphics Package
grDevices	The R Graphics Devices and Support for Colours
	and Fonts
grid	The Grid Graphics Package
KernSmooth	Functions for Kernel Smoothing Supporting Wand
	& Jones (1995)
lattice	Trellis Graphics for R
MASS	Support Functions and Datasets for Venables and
	Ripley's MASS
Matrix	Sparse and Dense Matrix Classes and Methods
methods	Formal Methods and Classes
mgcv	Mixed GAM Computation Vehicle with GCV/AIC/REML
	Smoothness Estimation
nlme	Linear and Nonlinear Mixed Effects Models

nnet	Feed-Forward Neural Networks and Multinomial Log-Linear Models
parallel	Support for Parallel computation in R
rpart	Recursive Partitioning and Regression Trees
spatial	Functions for Kriging and Point Pattern Analysis
splines	Regression Spline Functions and Classes
stats	The R Stats Package
stats4	Statistical Functions using S4 Classes
survival	Survival Analysis
tcltk	Tcl/Tk Interface
tools	Tools for Package Development
utils	The R Utils Package

Get all packages currently loaded in the R environment

```
search()
```

When we execute the above code, it produces the following result. It may vary depending on the local settings of your pc.

```
[1] ".GlobalEnv"      "package:stats"   "package:graphics"
[4]          "package:grDevices"          "package:utils"
"package:datasets"
[7] "package:methods"  "Autoloads"       "package:base"
```

Install a New Package:

There are two ways to add new R packages. One is installing directly from the CRAN directory and another is downloading the package to your local system and installing it manually.

Install directly from CRAN

The following command gets the packages directly from CRAN webpage and installs the package in the R environment. You may be prompted to choose a nearest mirror. Choose the one appropriate to your location.

```
install.packages("Package Name")
```

```
# Install the package named "XML".
install.packages("XML")
```

Install package manually

Go to the link R Packages to download the package needed. Save the package as a **.zip** file in a suitable location in the local system.

Now you can run the following command to install this package in the R environment.

```
install.packages(file_name_with_path, repos = NULL, type = "source")
```

```
# Install the package named "XML"
install.packages("E:/XML_3.98-1.3.zip", repos = NULL, type = "source")
```

Load Package to Library

Before a package can be used in the code, it must be loaded to the current R environment. You also need to load a package that is already installed previously but not available in the current environment.

A package is loaded using the following command –

```
library("package Name", lib.loc = "path to library")

# Load the package named "XML"
install.packages("E:/XML_3.98-1.3.zip", repos = NULL,
type = "source")
```

R - Data Reshaping

Data Reshaping in R is about changing the way data is organized into rows and columns. Most of the time data processing in R is done by taking the input data as a data frame. It is easy to extract data from the rows and columns of a data frame but there are situations when we need the data frame in a format that is different from format in which we received it. R has many functions to split, merge and change the rows to columns and vice-versa in a data frame.

Joining Columns and Rows in a Data Frame

We can join multiple vectors to create a data frame using the **cbind()**function. Also we can merge two data frames using **rbind()** function.

```
# Create vector objects.
city <- c("Tampa","Seattle","Hartford","Denver")
state <- c("FL","WA","CT","CO")
zipcode <- c(33602,98104,06161,80294)

# Combine above three vectors into one data frame.
addresses <- cbind(city,state,zipcode)

# Print a header.
cat("# # # # The First data frame\n")

# Print the data frame.
print(addresses)

# Create another data frame with similar columns
new.address <- data.frame(
  city = c("Lowry","Charlotte"),
```

```
  state = c("CO","FL"),
  zipcode = c("80230","33949"),
  stringsAsFactors = FALSE
)

# Print a header.
cat("# # # The Second data frame\n")

# Print the data frame.
print(new.address)

# Combine rows form both the data frames.
all.addresses <- rbind(addresses,new.address)

# Print a header.
cat("# # # The combined data frame\n")

# Print the result.
print(all.addresses)
```

When we execute the above code, it produces the following result –

```
# # # # The First data frame
   city     state zipcode
[1,] "Tampa"   "FL" "33602"
[2,] "Seattle" "WA" "98104"
[3,] "Hartford" "CT" "6161"
[4,] "Denver"  "CO" "80294"

# # # The Second data frame
    city     state zipcode
1   Lowry    CO    80230
2   Charlotte FL   33949
```

```
# # # The combined data frame
     city    state zipcode
1    Tampa   FL    33602
2    Seattle WA    98104
3    Hartford CT   6161
4    Denver  CO    80294
5    Lowry   CO    80230
6    Charlotte FL  33949
```

Merging Data Frames

We can merge two data frames by using the **merge()** function. The data frames must have same column names on which the merging happens.

In the example below, we consider the data sets about Diabetes in Pima Indian Women available in the library names "MASS". we merge the two data sets based on the values of blood pressure("bp") and body mass index("bmi"). On choosing these two columns for merging, the records where values of these two variables match in both data sets are combined together to form a single data frame.

```
library(MASS)
merged.Pima <- merge(x = Pima.te, y = Pima.tr,
   by.x = c("bp", "bmi"),
   by.y = c("bp", "bmi")
)
print(merged.Pima)
nrow(merged.Pima)
```

When we execute the above code, it produces the following result −

	bp	bmi	npreg.x	glu.x	skin.x	ped.x	age.x	type.x	npreg.y	glu.y	skin.y	ped.y
1	60	33.8	1	117	23	0.466	27	No	2	125	20	0.088
2	64	29.7	2	75	24	0.370	33	No	2	100	23	0.368
3	64	31.2	5	189	33	0.583	29	Yes	3	158	13	0.295
4	64	33.2	4	117	27	0.230	24	No	1	96	27	0.289
5	66	38.1	3	115	39	0.150	28	No	1	114	36	0.289
6	68	38.5	2	100	25	0.324	26	No	7	129	49	0.439
7	70	27.4	1	116	28	0.204	21	No	0	124	20	0.254
8	70	33.1	4	91	32	0.446	22	No	9	123	44	0.374
9	70	35.4	9	124	33	0.282	34	No	6	134	23	0.542
10	72	25.6	1	157	21	0.123	24	No	4	99	17	0.294
11	72	37.7	5	95	33	0.370	27	No	6	103	32	0.324
12	74	25.9	9	134	33	0.460	81	No	8	126	38	0.162
13	74	25.9	1	95	21	0.673	36	No	8	126	38	0.162
14	78	27.6	5	88	30	0.258	37	No	6	125	31	0.565
15	78	27.6	10	122	31	0.512	45	No	6	125	31	0.565
16	78	39.4	2	112	50	0.175	24	No	4	112	40	0.236

```
17 88 34.5      1   117    24 0.403   40    Yes      4   127
11 0.598
   age.y type.y
1    31   No
2    21   No
3    24   No
4    21   No
5    21   No
6    43   Yes
7    36   Yes
8    40   No
9    29   Yes
10   28   No
11   55   No
12   39   No
13   39   No
14   49   Yes
15   49   Yes
16   38   No
17   28   No
[1] 17
```

Melting and Casting

One of the most interesting aspects of R programming is about changing the shape of the data in multiple steps to get a desired shape. The functions used to do this are called **melt()** and **cast()**.

We consider the dataset called ships present in the library called "MASS".

```
library(MASS)
print(ships)
```

When we execute the above code, it produces the following result –

	type	year	period	service	incidents
1	A	60	60	127	0
2	A	60	75	63	0
3	A	65	60	1095	3
4	A	65	75	1095	4
5	A	70	60	1512	6
....					
....					
8	A	75	75	2244	11
9	B	60	60	44882	39
10	B	60	75	17176	29
11	B	65	60	28609	58
....					
....					
17	C	60	60	1179	1
18	C	60	75	552	1
19	C	65	60	781	0
....					
....					

Melt the Data

Now we melt the data to organize it, converting all columns other than type and year into multiple rows.

```
molten.ships <- melt(ships, id = c("type","year"))
print(molten.ships)
```

When we execute the above code, it produces the following result −

	type	year	variable	value
1	A	60	period	60
2	A	60	period	75
3	A	65	period	60
4	A	65	period	75
....				
....				
9	B	60	period	60
10	B	60	period	75
11	B	65	period	60
12	B	65	period	75
13	B	70	period	60
....				
....				
41	A	60	service	127
42	A	60	service	63
43	A	65	service	1095
....				
....				
70	D	70	service	1208
71	D	75	service	0
72	D	75	service	2051
73	E	60	service	45
74	E	60	service	0
75	E	65	service	789
....				
....				
101	C	70	incidents	6
102	C	70	incidents	2
103	C	75	incidents	0
104	C	75	incidents	1
105	D	60	incidents	0

```
106   D   60   incidents   0
............
............
```

Cast the Molten Data

We can cast the molten data into a new form where the aggregate of each type of ship for each year is created. It is done using the **cast()** function.

```
recasted.ship          <-          cast(molten.ships,
type+year~variable,sum)
print(recasted.ship)
```

When we execute the above code, it produces the following result –

	type	year	period	service	incidents
1	A	60	135	190	0
2	A	65	135	2190	7
3	A	70	135	4865	24
4	A	75	135	2244	11
5	B	60	135	62058	68
6	B	65	135	48979	111
7	B	70	135	20163	56
8	B	75	135	7117	18
9	C	60	135	1731	2
10	C	65	135	1457	1
11	C	70	135	2731	8
12	C	75	135	274	1
13	D	60	135	356	0
14	D	65	135	480	0
15	D	70	135	1557	13
16	D	75	135	2051	4

17	E	60	135	45	0
18	E	65	135	1226	14
19	E	70	135	3318	17
20	E	75	135	542	1

R - CSV Files

In R, we can read data from files stored outside the R environment. We can also write data into files which will be stored and accessed by the operating system. R can read and write into various file formats like csv, excel, xml etc.

In this chapter we will learn to read data from a csv file and then write data into a csv file. The file should be present in current working directory so that R can read it. Of course we can also set our own directory and read files from there.

Getting and Setting the Working Directory

You can check which directory the R workspace is pointing to using the **getwd()**function. You can also set a new working directory using **setwd()**function.

```
# Get and print current working directory.
print(getwd())

# Set current working directory.
setwd("/web/com")

# Get and print current working directory.
print(getwd())
```

When we execute the above code, it produces the following result −

```
[1] "/web/com/1441086124_2016"
[1] "/web/com"
```

This result depends on your OS and your current directory where you are working.

Input as CSV File:

The csv file is a text file in which the values in the columns are separated by a comma. Let's consider the following data present in the file named **input.csv**.

You can create this file using windows notepad by copying and pasting this data. Save the file as **input.csv** using the save As All files(*.*) option in notepad.

```
id,name,salary,start_date,dept
1,Rick,623.3,2012-01-01,IT
2,Dan,515.2,2013-09-23,Operations
3,Michelle,611,2014-11-15,IT
4,Ryan,729,2014-05-11,HR
5,Gary,843.25,2015-03-27,Finance
6,Nina,578,2013-05-21,IT
7,Simon,632.8,2013-07-30,Operations
8,Guru,722.5,2014-06-17,Finance
```

Reading a CSV File

Following is a simple example of **read.csv()** function to read a CSV file available in your current working directory −

```
data <- read.csv("input.csv")
print(data)
```

When we execute the above code, it produces the following result −

	id	name	salary	start_date	dept
1	1	Rick	623.30	2012-01-01	IT

2	2	Dan	515.20	2013-09-23	Operations
3	3	Michelle	611.00	2014-11-15	IT
4	4	Ryan	729.00	2014-05-11	HR
5	NA	Gary	843.25	2015-03-27	Finance
6	6	Nina	578.00	2013-05-21	IT
7	7	Simon	632.80	2013-07-30	Operations
8	8	Guru	722.50	2014-06-17	Finance

Analyzing the CSV File

By default the **read.csv()** function gives the output as a data frame. This can be easily checked as follows. Also we can check the number of columns and rows.

```
data <- read.csv("input.csv")

print(is.data.frame(data))
print(ncol(data))
print(nrow(data))
```

When we execute the above code, it produces the following result −

```
[1] TRUE
[1] 5
[1] 8
```

Once we read data in a data frame, we can apply all the functions applicable to data frames as explained in subsequent section.

Get the maximum salary:

```
# Create a data frame.
data <- read.csv("input.csv")

# Get the max salary from data frame.
sal <- max(data$salary)
print(sal)
```

When we execute the above code, it produces the following result −

```
[1] 843.25
```

Get the details of the person with max salary

We can fetch rows meeting specific filter criteria similar to a SQL where clause.

```
# Create a data frame.
data <- read.csv("input.csv")

# Get the max salary from data frame.
sal <- max(data$salary)

# Get the person detail having max salary.
retval <- subset(data, salary == max(salary))
print(retval)
```

When we execute the above code, it produces the following result −

```
  id name salary start_date   dept
5 NA  Gary 843.25 2015-03-27 Finance
```

Get all the people working in IT department

```
# Create a data frame.
data <- read.csv("input.csv")

retval <- subset( data, dept == "IT")
print(retval)
```

When we execute the above code, it produces the following result −

```
   id name     salary start_date dept
1  1  Rick     623.3  2012-01-01 IT
3  3  Michelle 611.0  2014-11-15 IT
6  6  Nina     578.0  2013-05-21 IT
```

Get the persons in IT department whose salary is greater than 600

```
# Create a data frame.
data <- read.csv("input.csv")

info <- subset(data, salary > 600 & dept == "IT")
print(info)
```

When we execute the above code, it produces the following result −

```
   id name     salary start_date dept
1  1  Rick     623.3  2012-01-01 IT
3  3  Michelle 611.0  2014-11-15 IT
```

Get the people who joined on or after 2014

```
# Create a data frame.
data <- read.csv("input.csv")

retval <- subset(data, as.Date(start_date) >
as.Date("2014-01-01"))
print(retval)
```

When we execute the above code, it produces the following result −

```
   id name    salary start_date  dept
3  3  Michelle 611.00 2014-11-15  IT
4  4  Ryan    729.00 2014-05-11  HR
5  NA Gary    843.25 2015-03-27  Finance
8  8  Guru    722.50 2014-06-17  Finance
```

Writing into a CSV File

R can create csv file form existing data frame. The **write.csv()** function is used to create the csv file. This file gets created in the working directory.

```
# Create a data frame.
data <- read.csv("input.csv")
retval <- subset(data, as.Date(start_date) > as.Date("2014-01-01"))

# Write filtered data into a new file.
write.csv(retval,"output.csv")
newdata <- read.csv("output.csv")
print(newdata)
```

When we execute the above code, it produces the following result –

X	id	name	salary	start_date	dept
1 3	3	Michelle	611.00	2014-11-15	IT
2 4	4	Ryan	729.00	2014-05-11	HR
3 5	NA	Gary	843.25	2015-03-27	Finance
4 8	8	Guru	722.50	2014-06-17	Finance

Here the column X comes from the data set newper. This can be dropped using additional parameters while writing the file.

```
# Create a data frame.
data <- read.csv("input.csv")
retval <- subset(data, as.Date(start_date) > as.Date("2014-01-01"))

# Write filtered data into a new file.
write.csv(retval,"output.csv", row.names = FALSE)
newdata <- read.csv("output.csv")
print(newdata)
```

When we execute the above code, it produces the following result –

id	name	salary	start_date	dept
1	3	Michelle	611.00	2014-11-15	IT
2	4	Ryan	729.00	2014-05-11	HR
3	NA	Gary	843.25	2015-03-27	Finance
4	8	Guru	722.50	2014-06-17	Finance

R - Excel File

Microsoft Excel is the most widely used spreadsheet program which stores data in the .xls or .xlsx format. R can read directly from these files using some excel specific packages. Few such packages are - XLConnect, xlsx, gdata etc. We will be using xlsx package. R can also write into excel file using this package.

Install xlsx Package

You can use the following command in the R console to install the "xlsx" package. It may ask to install some additional packages on which this package is dependent. Follow the same command with required package name to install the additional packages.

```
install.packages("xlsx")
```

Verify and Load the "xlsx" Package

Use the following command to verify and load the "xlsx" package.

```
# Verify the package is installed.
any(grepl("xlsx",installed.packages()))

# Load the library into R workspace.
library("xlsx")
```

When the script is run we get the following output.

```
[1] TRUE
Loading required package: rJava
Loading required package: methods
Loading required package: xlsxjars
```

Input as xlsx File:

Open Microsoft excel. Copy and paste the following data in the work sheet named as sheet1.

id	name	salary	start_date	dept
1	Rick	623.3	1/1/2012	IT
2	Dan	515.2	9/23/2013	Operations
3	Michelle	611	11/15/2014	IT
4	Ryan	729	5/11/2014	HR
5	Gary	43.25	3/27/2015	Finance
6	Nina	578	5/21/2013	IT
7	Simon	632.8	7/30/2013	Operations
8	Guru	722.5	6/17/2014	Finance

Also copy and paste the following data to another worksheet and rename this worksheet to "city".

name	city
Rick	Seattle
Dan	Tampa
Michelle	Chicago
Ryan	Seattle
Gary	Houston
Nina	Boston
Simon	Mumbai
Guru	Dallas

Save the Excel file as "input.xlsx". You should save it in the current working directory of the R workspace.

Reading the Excel File

The input.xlsx is read by using the **read.xlsx()** function as shown below. The result is stored as a data frame in the R environment.

```
# Read the first worksheet in the file input.xlsx.
data <- read.xlsx("input.xlsx", sheetIndex = 1)
print(data)
```

When we execute the above code, it produces the following result –

	id,	name,	salary,	start_date,	dept
1	1	Rick	623.30	2012-01-01	IT
2	2	Dan	515.20	2013-09-23	Operations
3	3	Michelle	611.00	2014-11-15	IT
4	4	Ryan	729.00	2014-05-11	HR
5	NA	Gary	843.25	2015-03-27	Finance
6	6	Nina	578.00	2013-05-21	IT
7	7	Simon	632.80	2013-07-30	Operations
8	8	Guru	722.50	2014-06-17	Finance

R - Binary Files

A binary file is a file that contains information stored only in form of bits and bytes.(0's and 1's). They are not human readable as the bytes in it translate to characters and symbols which contain many other non-printable characters. Attempting to read a binary file using any text editor will show characters like Ø and ð.

The binary file has to be read by specific programs to be useable. For example, the binary file of a Microsoft Word program can be read to a human readable form only by the Word program. Which indicates that, besides the human readable text, there is a lot more information like formatting of characters and page numbers etc., which are also stored along with alphanumeric characters. And finally a binary file is a continuous sequence of bytes. The line break we see in a text file is a character joining first line to the next.

Sometimes, the data generated by other programs are required to be processed by R as a binary file. Also R is required to create binary files which can be shared with other programs.

R has two functions **WriteBin()** and **readBin()** to create and read binary files.

Syntax

```
writeBin(object, con)
readBin(con, what, n )
```

Following is the description of the parameters used −

- **con** is the connection object to read or write the binary file.

- **object** is the binary file which to be written.

- **what** is the mode like character, integer etc. representing the bytes to be read.

- **n** is the number of bytes to read from the binary file.

Example

We consider the R inbuilt data "mtcars". First we create a csv file from it and convert it to a binary file and store it as a OS file. Next we read this binary file created into R.

Writing the Binary File

We read the data frame "mtcars" as a csv file and then write it as a binary file to the OS.

```
# Read the "mtcars" data frame as a csv file and store only the columns
   "cyl", "am" and "gear".
write.table(mtcars,   file   =   "mtcars.csv",row.names   =
FALSE, na = "",
   col.names = TRUE, sep = ",")

# Store 5 records from the csv file as a new data frame.
new.mtcars <- read.table("mtcars.csv",sep = ",",header =
TRUE,nrows = 5)

# Create a connection object to write the binary file using
mode "wb".
write.filename = file("/web/com/binmtcars.dat", "wb")

# Write the column names of the data frame to the
connection object.
```

```
writeBin(colnames(new.mtcars), write.filename)

# Write the records in each of the column to the file.
writeBin(c(new.mtcars$cyl,new.mtcars$am,new.mtcars$ge
ar), write.filename)

# Close the file for writing so that it can be read by other
program.
close(write.filename)
```

Reading the Binary File

The binary file created above stores all the data as continuous bytes. So we will read it by choosing appropriate values of column names as well as the column values.

```
# Create a connection object to read the file in binary mode
using "rb".
read.filename <- file("/web/com/binmtcars.dat", "rb")

# First read the column names. n = 3 as we have 3 columns.
column.names <- readBin(read.filename, character(), n =
3)

# Next read the column values. n = 18 as we have 3 column
names and 15 values.
read.filename <- file("/web/com/binmtcars.dat", "rb")
bindata <- readBin(read.filename, integer(), n = 18)

# Print the data.
print(bindata)
```

```
# Read the values from 4th byte to 8th byte which
represents "cyl".
cyldata = bindata[4:8]
print(cyldata)

# Read the values form 9th byte to 13th byte which
represents "am".
amdata = bindata[9:13]
print(amdata)

# Read the values form 9th byte to 13th byte which
represents "gear".
geardata = bindata[14:18]
print(geardata)

# Combine all the read values to a dat frame.
finaldata = cbind(cyldata, amdata, geardata)
colnames(finaldata) = column.names
print(finaldata)
```

When we execute the above code, it produces the
following result and chart –

```
[1]    7108963 1728081249    7496037         6        6
4
[7]      6     8     1     1     1     0
[13]     0     4     4     4     3     3

[1] 6 6 4 6 8

[1] 1 1 1 0 0

[1] 4 4 4 3 3
```

```
      cyl am gear
[1,]   6  1   4
[2,]   6  1   4
[3,]   4  1   4
[4,]   6  0   3
[5,]   8  0   3
```

As we can see, we got the original data back by reading the binary file in R.

R - XML Files

XML is a file format which shares both the file format and the data on the World Wide Web, intranets, and elsewhere using standard ASCII text. It stands for Extensible Markup Language (XML). Similar to HTML it contains markup tags. But unlike HTML where the markup tag describes structure of the page, in xml the markup tags describe the meaning of the data contained into he file.

You can read a xml file in R using the "XML" package. This package can be installed using following command.

```
install.packages("XML")
```

Input Data:

Create a XMl file by copying the below data into a text editor like notepad. Save the file with a **.xml** extension and choosing the file type as **all files(*.*)**.

```
<RECORDS>
 <EMPLOYEE>
  <ID>1</ID>
  <NAME>Rick</NAME>
  <SALARY>623.3</SALARY>
  <STARTDATE>1/1/2012</STARTDATE>
  <DEPT>IT</DEPT>
 </EMPLOYEE>

 <EMPLOYEE>
  <ID>2</ID>
  <NAME>Dan</NAME>
  <SALARY>515.2</SALARY>
  <STARTDATE>9/23/2013</STARTDATE>
  <DEPT>Operations</DEPT>
```

```
</EMPLOYEE>

<EMPLOYEE>
  <ID>3</ID>
  <NAME>Michelle</NAME>
  <SALARY>611</SALARY>
  <STARTDATE>11/15/2014</STARTDATE>
  <DEPT>IT</DEPT>
</EMPLOYEE>

<EMPLOYEE>
  <ID>4</ID>
  <NAME>Ryan</NAME>
  <SALARY>729</SALARY>
  <STARTDATE>5/11/2014</STARTDATE>
  <DEPT>HR</DEPT>
</EMPLOYEE>

<EMPLOYEE>
  <ID>5</ID>
  <NAME>Gary</NAME>
  <SALARY>843.25</SALARY>
  <STARTDATE>3/27/2015</STARTDATE>
  <DEPT>Finance</DEPT>
</EMPLOYEE>

<EMPLOYEE>
  <ID>6</ID>
  <NAME>Nina</NAME>
  <SALARY>578</SALARY>
  <STARTDATE>5/21/2013</STARTDATE>
  <DEPT>IT</DEPT>
</EMPLOYEE>

<EMPLOYEE>
```

```
    <ID>7</ID>
    <NAME>Simon</NAME>
    <SALARY>632.8</SALARY>
    <STARTDATE>7/30/2013</STARTDATE>
    <DEPT>Operations</DEPT>
  </EMPLOYEE>

  <EMPLOYEE>
    <ID>8</ID>
    <NAME>Guru</NAME>
    <SALARY>722.5</SALARY>
    <STARTDATE>6/17/2014</STARTDATE>
    <DEPT>Finance</DEPT>
  </EMPLOYEE>

</RECORDS>
```

Reading XML File

The xml file is read by R using the function **xmlParse()**. It is stored as a list in R.

```
# Load the package required to read XML files.
library("XML")

# Also load the other required package.
library("methods")

# Give the input file name to the function.
result <- xmlParse(file = "input.xml")

# Print the result.
print(result)
```

When we execute the above code, it produces the following result −

```
1
Rick
623.3
1/1/2012
IT

2
Dan
515.2
9/23/2013
Operations

3
Michelle
611
11/15/2014
IT

4
Ryan
729
5/11/2014
HR

5
Gary
843.25
3/27/2015
Finance

6
Nina
```

```
578
5/21/2013
IT

7
Simon
632.8
7/30/2013
Operations

8
Guru
722.5
6/17/2014
Finance
```

Get Number of Nodes Present in XML File:

```
# Load the packages required to read XML files.
library("XML")
library("methods")

# Give the input file name to the function.
result <- xmlParse(file = "input.xml")

# Exract the root node form the xml file.
rootnode <- xmlRoot(result)

# Find number of nodes in the root.
rootsize <- xmlSize(rootnode)

# Print the result.
```

```
print(rootsize)
```

When we execute the above code, it produces the following result –

```
output
[1] 8
```

Details of the First Node

Let's look at the first record of the parsed file. It will give us an idea of the various elements present in the top level node.

```
# Load the packages required to read XML files.
library("XML")
library("methods")

# Give the input file name to the function.
result <- xmlParse(file = "input.xml")

# Exract the root node form the xml file.
rootnode <- xmlRoot(result)

# Print the result.
print(rootnode[1])
```

When we execute the above code, it produces the following result –

```
$EMPLOYEE
  1
  Rick
  623.3
```

```
1/1/2012
IT
```

```
attr(,"class")
[1] "XMLInternalNodeList" "XMLNodeList"
```

Get Different Elements of a Node:

```
# Load the packages required to read XML files.
library("XML")
library("methods")

# Give the input file name to the function.
result <- xmlParse(file = "input.xml")

# Exract the root node form the xml file.
rootnode <- xmlRoot(result)

# Get the first element of the first node.
print(rootnode[[1]][[1]])

# Get the fifth element of the first node.
print(rootnode[[1]][[5]])

# Get the second element of the third node.
print(rootnode[[3]][[2]])
```

When we execute the above code, it produces the following result –

```
1
IT
Michelle
```

XML to Data Frame:

To handle the data effectively in large files we read the data in the xml file as a data frame. Then process the data frame for data analysis.

```
# Load the packages required to read XML files.
library("XML")
library("methods")

# Convert the input xml file to a data frame.
xmldataframe <- xmlToDataFrame("input.xml")
print(xmldataframe)
```

When we execute the above code, it produces the following result –

	ID	NAME	SALARY	STARTDATE	DEPT
1	1	Rick	623.30	2012-01-01	IT
2	2	Dan	515.20	2013-09-23	Operations
3	3	Michelle	611.00	2014-11-15	IT
4	4	Ryan	729.00	2014-05-11	HR
5	NA	Gary	843.25	2015-03-27	Finance
6	6	Nina	578.00	2013-05-21	IT
7	7	Simon	632.80	2013-07-30	Operations
8	8	Guru	722.50	2014-06-17	Finance

As the data is now available as a dataframe we can use data frame related function to read and manipulate the file.

R - JSON Files

JSON file stores data as text in human-readable format. Json stands for JavaScript Object Notation. R can read JSON files using the rjson package.

Install rjson Package

In the R console, you can issue the following command to install the rjson package.

```
install.packages("rjson")
```

Input Data

Create a JSON file by copying the below data into a text editor like notepad. Save the file with a **.json** extension and choosing the file type as **all files(*.*)**.

```
{
   "ID":["1","2","3","4","5","6","7","8" ],

"Name":["Rick","Dan","Michelle","Ryan","Gary","Nina","Simon","Guru" ],

"Salary":["623.3","515.2","611","729","843.25","578","632.8","722.5" ],

   "StartDate":[
"1/1/2012","9/23/2013","11/15/2014","5/11/2014","3/27/2015","5/21/2013",
   "7/30/2013","6/17/2014"],
   "Dept":[
"IT","Operations","IT","HR","Finance","IT","Operations","Finance"]
```

```
}
```

Read the JSON File

The JSON file is read by R using the function from **JSON()**. It is stored as a list in R.

```
# Load the package required to read JSON files.
library("rjson")

# Give the input file name to the function.
result <- fromJSON(file = "input.json")

# Print the result.
print(result)
```

When we execute the above code, it produces the following result −

```
$ID
[1] "1"  "2"  "3"  "4"  "5"  "6"  "7"  "8"

$Name
[1] "Rick"    "Dan"     "Michelle" "Ryan"    "Gary"
"Nina"    "Simon"   "Guru"

$Salary
[1] "623.3"  "515.2"  "611"    "729"    "843.25" "578"
"632.8"  "722.5"

$StartDate
[1] "1/1/2012"  "9/23/2013" "11/15/2014" "5/11/2014"
"3/27/2015" "5/21/2013"
  "7/30/2013" "6/17/2014"
```

```
$Dept
[1] "IT"       "Operations" "IT"       "HR"       "Finance"
"IT"
   "Operations" "Finance"
```

Convert JSON to a Data Frame

We can convert the extracted data above to a R data frame
for further analysis using the **as.data.frame()** function.

```
# Load the package required to read JSON files.
library("rjson")

# Give the input file name to the function.
result <- fromJSON(file = "input.json")

# Convert JSON file to a data frame.
json_data_frame <- as.data.frame(result)

print(json_data_frame)
```

When we execute the above code, it produces the
following result –

	id,	name,	salary,	start_date,	dept
1	1	Rick	623.30	2012-01-01	IT
2	2	Dan	515.20	2013-09-23	Operations
3	3	Michelle	611.00	2014-11-15	IT
4	4	Ryan	729.00	2014-05-11	HR
5	NA	Gary	843.25	2015-03-27	Finance
6	6	Nina	578.00	2013-05-21	IT
7	7	Simon	632.80	2013-07-30	Operations
8	8	Guru	722.50	2014-06-17	Finance

R - Web Data

Many websites provide data for consumption by its users. For example the World Health Organization(WHO) provides reports on health and medical information in the form of CSV, txt and XML files. Using R programs, we can programmatically extract specific data from such websites. Some packages in R which are used to scrap data form the web are – "RCurl","XML", and "stringr". They are used to connect to the URL's, identify required links for the files and download them to the local environment.

Install R Packages:

The following packages are required for processing the URL's and links to the files. If they are not available in your R Environment, you can install them using following commands.

```
install.packages("RCurl")
install.packages("XML")
install.packages("stringr")
install.packages("plyr")
```

Input Data:

We will visit the URL weather data and download the CSV files using R for the year 2015.

Example:

We will use the function **getHTMLLinks()** to gather the URLs of the files. Then we will use the function **download.file()** to save the files to the local system. As we will be applying the same code again and again for multiple files, we will create a function to be called multiple times.

The filenames are passed as parameters in form of a R list object to this function.

```
# Read the URL.
url <- "http://www.geos.ed.ac.uk/~weather/jcmb_ws/"

# Gather the html links present in the webpage.
links <- getHTMLLinks(url)

# Identify only the links which point to the JCMB 2015
files.
filenames <- links[str_detect(links, "JCMB_2015")]

# Store the file names as a list.
filenames_list <- as.list(filenames)

# Create a function to download the files by passing the
URL and filename list.
downloadcsv <- function (mainurl,filename) {
    filedetails <- str_c(mainurl,filename)
    download.file(filedetails,filename)
}

# Now apply the l_ply function and save the files into the
current R working directory.
l_ply(filenames,downloadcsv,mainurl =
"http://www.geos.ed.ac.uk/~weather/jcmb_ws/")
```

Verify the File Download

After running the above code, you can locate the following files in the current R working directory.

```
"JCMB_2015.csv"                "JCMB_2015_Apr.csv"
"JCMB_2015_Feb.csv" "JCMB_2015_Jan.csv"
 "JCMB_2015_Mar.csv"
```

R - Databases

The data is Relational database systems are stored in a normalized format. So, to carry out statistical computing we will need very advanced and complex Sql queries. But R can connect easily to many relational databases like MySql, Oracle, Sql server etc. and fetch records from them as a data frame. Once the data is available in the R environment, it becomes a normal R data set and can be manipulated or analyzed using all the powerful packages and functions.

In this tutorial we will be using MySql as our reference database for connecting to R.

RMySQL Package:

R has a built-in package named "RMySQL" which provides native connectivity between with MySql database. You can install this package in the R environment using the following command.

```
install.packages("RMySQL")
```

Connecting R to MySql:

Once the package is installed we create a connection object in R to connect to the database. It takes the username, password, database name and host name as input.

```
# Create a connection Object to MySQL database.
# We will connect to the sampel database named "sakila"
that comes with MySql installation.
```

```
mysqlconnection = dbConnect(MySQL(), user = 'root',
password = '', dbname = 'sakila',
  host = 'localhost')

# List the tables available in this database.
dbListTables(mysqlconnection)
```

When we execute the above code, it produces the following result –

```
[1] "actor"                    "actor_info"
[3] "address"                  "category"
[5] "city"                     "country"
[7] "customer"                 "customer_list"
[9] "film"                     "film_actor"
[11] "film_category"           "film_list"
[13] "film_text"               "inventory"
[15] "language"                "nicer_but_slower_film_list"
[17] "payment"                 "rental"
[19] "sales_by_film_category"  "sales_by_store"
[21] "staff"                   "staff_list"
[23] "store"
```

Querying the Tables

We can query the database tables in MySql using the function **dbSendQuery()**. The query gets executed in MySql and the result set is returned using the R **fetch()**function. Finally it is stored as a data frame in R.

```
# Query the "actor" tables to get all the rows.
result = dbSendQuery(mysqlconnection, "select * from
actor")
```

```
# Store the result in a R data frame object. n = 5 is used to
fetch first 5 rows.
data.frame = fetch(result, n = 5)
print(data.fame)
```

When we execute the above code, it produces the
following result −

	actor_id	first_name	last_name	last_update
1	1	PENELOPE	GUINESS	2006-02-15 04:34:33
2	2	NICK	WAHLBERG	2006-02-15 04:34:33
3	3	ED	CHASE	2006-02-15 04:34:33
4	4	JENNIFER	DAVIS	2006-02-15 04:34:33
5	5	JOHNNY	LOLLOBRIGIDA	2006-02-15 04:34:33

Query with Filter Clause

We can pass any valid select query to get the result.

```
result = dbSendQuery(mysqlconnection, "select * from
actor where last_name = 'TORN'")

# Fetch all the records(with n = -1) and store it as a data
frame.
data.frame = fetch(result, n = -1)
print(data)
```

When we execute the above code, it produces the following result –

	actor_id	first_name	last_name	last_update
1	18	DAN	TORN	2006-02-15 04:34:33
2	94	KENNETH	TORN	2006-02-15 04:34:33
3	102	WALTER	TORN	2006-02-15 04:34:33

Updating Rows in the Tables

We can update the rows in a Mysql table by passing the update query to the dbSendQuery() function.

```
dbSendQuery(mysqlconnection, "update mtcars set disp = 168.5 where hp = 110")
```

After executing the above code we can see the table updated in the MySql Environment.

Inserting Data into the Tables

```
dbSendQuery(mysqlconnection,
  "insert into mtcars(row_names, mpg, cyl, disp, hp, drat, wt, qsec, vs, am, gear, carb)
  values('New Mazda RX4 Wag', 21, 6, 168.5, 110, 3.9, 2.875, 17.02, 0, 1, 4, 4)"
)
```

After executing the above code we can see the row inserted into the table in the MySql Environment.

Creating Tables in MySql:

We can create tables in the MySql using the function **dbWriteTable()**. It overwrites the table if it already exists and takes a data frame as input.

```
# Create the connection object to the database where we
want to create the table.
mysqlconnection = dbConnect(MySQL(), user = 'root',
password = '', dbname = 'sakila',
  host = 'localhost')

# Use the R data frame "mtcars" to create the table in
MySql.
# All the rows of mtcars are taken inot MySql.
dbWriteTable(mysqlconnection, "mtcars", mtcars[, ],
overwrite = TRUE)
```

After executing the above code we can see the table created in the MySql Environment.

Dropping Tables in MySql

We can drop the tables in MySql database passing the drop table statement into the dbSendQuery() in the same way we used it for querying data from tables.

```
dbSendQuery(mysqlconnection, 'drop table if exists
mtcars')
```

After executing the above code we can see the table is dropped in the MySql Environment.

R Programming Charts & Graphs

R Programming language has various libraries for creating charts and graphs. In next chapter we will look at some of the ways R can display information graphically. This is a basic introduction to some of the basic plotting commands. It is assumed that you know how to enter data or read data files which is covered in the previous chapters, and it is assumed that you are familiar with the different data types.

R - Pie Charts

R Programming language has numerous libraries to create charts and graphs. A pie-chart is a representation of values as slices of a circle with different colors. The slices are labeled and the numbers corresponding to each slice is also represented in the chart.

In R the pie chart is created using the **pie()** function which takes positive numbers as a vector input. The additional parameters are used to control labels, color, title etc.

Syntax:

The basic syntax for creating a pie-chart using the R is –

pie(x, labels, radius, main, col, clockwise)

Following is the description of the parameters used –

- **x** is a vector containing the numeric values used in the pie chart.

- **labels** is used to give description to the slices.

- **radius** indicates the radius of the circle of the pie chart.(value between −1 and +1).

- **main** indicates the title of the chart.

- **col** indicates the color palette.

- **clockwise** is a logical value indicating if the slices are drawn clockwise or anti clockwise.

Example

A very simple pie-chart is created using just the input vector and labels. The below script will create and save the pie chart in the current R working directory.

```
# Create data for the graph.
x <- c(21, 62, 10, 53)
labels <- c("London", "New York", "Singapore", "Mumbai")

# Give the chart file a name.
png(file = "city.jpg")

# Plot the chart.
pie(x,labels)

# Save the file.
dev.off()
```

When we execute the above code, it produces the following result −

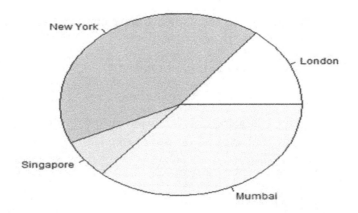

Pie Chart Title and Colors:

We can expand the features of the chart by adding more parameters to the function. We will use parameter **main** to add a title to the chart and another parameter is **col**which will make use of rainbow colour pallet while drawing the chart. The length of the pallet should be same as the number of values we have for the chart. Hence we use length(x).

Example:

The below script will create and save the pie chart in the current R working directory.

```
# Create data for the graph.
x <- c(21, 62, 10, 53)
labels <- c("London", "New York", "Singapore", "Mumbai")

# Give the chart file a name.
png(file = "city_title_colours.jpg")

# Plot the chart with title and rainbow color pallet.
pie(x, labels, main = "City pie chart", col = rainbow(length(x)))

# Save the file.
dev.off()
```

When we execute the above code, it produces the following result –

City pie chart

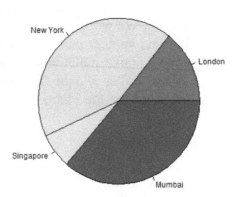

Slice Percentages and Chart Legend:

We can add slice percentage and a chart legend by creating additional chart variables.

```
# Create data for the graph.
x <- c(21, 62, 10,53)
labels <- c("London","New York","Singapore","Mumbai")

piepercent<- round(100*x/sum(x), 1)

# Give the chart file a name.
png(file = "city_percentage_legends.jpg")

# Plot the chart.
pie(x, labels = piepercent, main = "City pie chart",col =
rainbow(length(x)))
legend("topright",                          c("London","New
York","Singapore","Mumbai"), cex = 0.8,
  fill = rainbow(length(x)))
```

```
# Save the file.
dev.off()
```

When we execute the above code, it produces the following result –

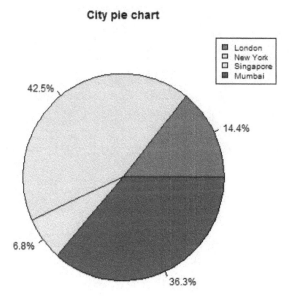

City pie chart

3D Pie Chart:

A pie chart with 3 dimensions can be drawn using additional packages. The package **plotrix** has a function called **pie3D()** that is used for this.

```
# Get the library.
```

```
library(plotrix)

# Create data for the graph.
x <- c(21, 62, 10,53)
lbl <- c("London","New York","Singapore","Mumbai")

# Give the chart file a name.
png(file = "3d_pie_chart.jpg")

# Plot the chart.
pie3D(x,labels = lbl,explode = 0.1, main = "Pie Chart of
Countries ")

# Save the file.
dev.off()
```

When we execute the above code, it produces the following result –

Pie Chart of Countries

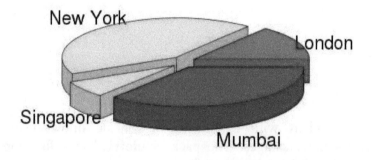

R - Bar Charts

A bar chart represents data in rectangular bars with length of the bar proportional to the value of the variable. R uses the function **barplot()** to create bar charts. R can draw both vertical and Horizontal bars in the bar chart. In bar chart each of the bars can be given different colors.

Syntax:

The basic syntax to create a bar-chart in R is −

barplot(H,xlab,ylab,main, names.arg,col)

Following is the description of the parameters used −

- **H** is a vector or matrix containing numeric values used in bar chart.
- **xlab** is the label for x axis.
- **ylab** is the label for y axis.
- **main** is the title of the bar chart.
- **names.arg** is a vector of names appearing under each bar.
- **col** is used to give colors to the bars in the graph.

Example:

A simple bar chart is created using just the input vector and the name of each bar.

The below script will create and save the bar chart in the current R working directory.

```
# Create the data for the chart
H <- c(7,12,28,3,41)
```

```
# Give the chart file a name
png(file = "barchart.png")

# Plot the bar chart
barplot(H)

# Save the file
dev.off()
```

When we execute above code, it produces following result –

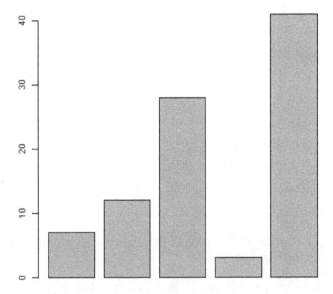

Bar Chart Labels, Title and Colors:

The features of the bar chart can be expanded by adding more parameters. The **main**parameter is used to add **title**. The **col** parameter is used to add colors to the bars. The **args.name** is a vector having same number of values as the input vector to describe the meaning of each bar.

Example

The below script will create and save the bar chart in the current R working directory.

```
# Create the data for the chart
H <- c(7,12,28,3,41)
M <- c("Mar","Apr","May","Jun","Jul")

# Give the chart file a name
png(file = "barchart_months_revenue.png")

# Plot the bar chart
barplot(H,names.arg=M,xlab="Month",ylab="Revenue",co
l="blue",
main="Revenue chart",border="red")

# Save the file
dev.off()
```

When we execute above code, it produces following result –

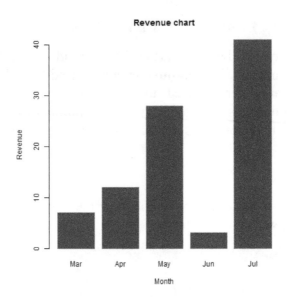

Group Bar Chart and Stacked Bar Chart:

We can create bar chart with groups of bars and stacks in each bar by using a matrix as input values.

More than two variables are represented as a matrix which is used to create the group bar chart and stacked bar chart.

```
# Create the input vectors.
colors = c("green","orange","brown")
months <- c("Mar","Apr","May","Jun","Jul")
regions <- c("East","West","North")

# Create the matrix of the values.
Values <- matrix(c(2,9,3,11,9,4,8,7,3,12,5,2,8,10,11), nrow
= 3, ncol = 5, byrow = TRUE)

# Give the chart file a name
```

```
png(file = "barchart_stacked.png")

# Create the bar chart
barplot(Values, main = "total revenue", names.arg =
months, xlab = "month", ylab = "revenue", col = colors)

# Add the legend to the chart
legend("topleft", regions, cex = 1.3, fill = colors)

# Save the file
dev.off()
```

When we execute above code, it produces following result
–

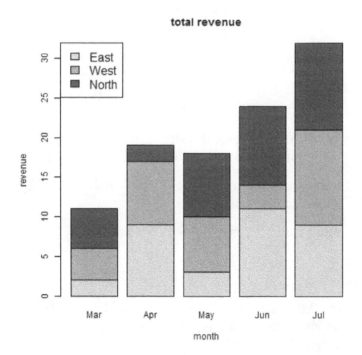

R - Boxplots

Boxplots are a measure of how well distributed is the data in a data set. It divides the data set into three quartiles. This graph represents the minimum, maximum, median, first quartile and third quartile in the data set. It is also useful in comparing the distribution of data across data sets by drawing boxplots for each of them.

Boxplots are created in R by using the **boxplot()** function.

Syntax

The basic syntax to create a boxplot in R is −

boxplot(x, data, notch, varwidth, names, main)

Following is the description of the parameters used −

- **x** is a vector or a formula.
- **data** is the data frame.
- **notch** is a logical value. Set as TRUE to draw a notch.
- **varwidth** is a logical value. Set as true to draw width of the box proportionate to the sample size.
- **names** are the group labels which will be printed under each boxplot.
- **main** is used to give a title to the graph.

Example

We use the data set "mtcars" available in the R environment to create a basic boxplot. Let's look at the columns "mpg" and "cyl" in mtcars.

```
input <- mtcars[,c('mpg','cyl')]
print(head(input))
```

When we execute above code, it produces following result –

```
            mpg cyl
Mazda RX4         21.0  6
Mazda RX4 Wag    21.0  6
Datsun 710       22.8  4
Hornet 4 Drive   21.4  6
Hornet Sportabout 18.7  8
Valiant          18.1  6
```

Creating the Boxplot

The below script will create a boxplot graph for the relation between mpg (miles per gallon) and cyl (number of cylinders).

```
# Give the chart file a name.
png(file = "boxplot.png")

# Plot the chart.
boxplot(mpg ~ cyl, data = mtcars, xlab = "Number of Cylinders",
   ylab = "Miles Per Gallon", main = "Mileage Data")

# Save the file.
dev.off()
```

When we execute the above code, it produces the following result –

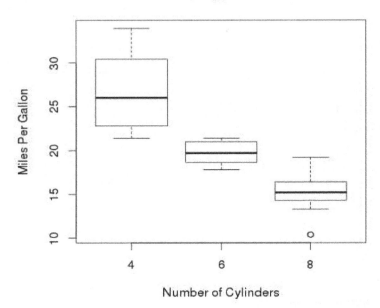

Boxplot with Notch:

We can draw boxplot with notch to find out how the medians of different data groups match with each other.

The below script will create a boxplot graph with notch for each of the data group.

```
# Give the chart file a name.
png(file = "boxplot_with_notch.png")

# Plot the chart.
boxplot(mpg ~ cyl, data = mtcars,
   xlab = "Number of Cylinders",
```

```
    ylab = "Miles Per Gallon",
    main = "Mileage Data",
    notch = TRUE,
    varwidth = TRUE,
    col = c("green","yellow","purple"),
    names = c("High","Medium","Low")
)
# Save the file.
dev.off()
```

When we execute the above code, it produces the following result –

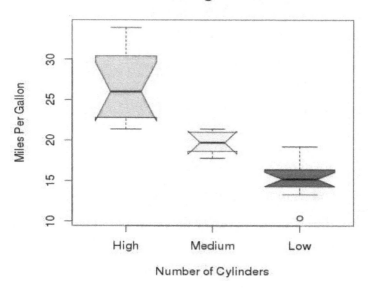

R - Histograms

A histogram represents the frequencies of values of a variable bucketed into ranges. Histogram is similar to bar chat but the difference is it groups the values into continuous ranges. Each bar in histogram represents the height of the number of values present in that range.

R creates histogram using **hist()** function. This function takes a vector as an input and uses some more parameters to plot histograms.

Syntax:

The basic syntax for creating a histogram using R is −

```
hist(v,main,xlab,xlim,ylim,breaks,col,border)
```

Following is the description of the parameters used −

- **v** is a vector containing numeric values used in histogram.
- **main** indicates title of the chart.
- **col** is used to set color of the bars.
- **border** is used to set border color of each bar.
- **xlab** is used to give description of x-axis.
- **xlim** is used to specify the range of values on the x-axis.
- **ylim** is used to specify the range of values on the y-axis.
- **breaks** is used to mention the width of each bar.

Example:

A simple histogram is created using input vector, label, col and border parameters.

The script given below will create and save the histogram in the current R working directory.

```
# Create data for the graph.
v <- c(9,13,21,8,36,22,12,41,31,33,19)

# Give the chart file a name.
png(file = "histogram.png")

# Create the histogram.
hist(v,xlab = "Weight",col = "yellow",border = "blue")

# Save the file.
dev.off()
```

When we execute the above code, it produces the following result −

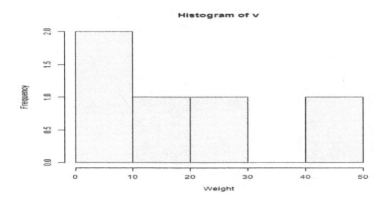

Range of X and Y values:

To specify the range of values allowed in X axis and Y axis, we can use the xlim and ylim parameters.

The width of each of the bar can be decided by using breaks.

```
# Create data for the graph.
v <- c(9,13,21,8,36,22,12,41,31,33,19)

# Give the chart file a name.
png(file = "histogram_lim_breaks.png")

# Create the histogram.
hist(v,xlab = "Weight",col = "green",border = "red", xlim =
c(0,40), ylim = c(0,5),
   breaks = 5)

# Save the file.
dev.off()
```

When we execute the above code, it produces the following result −

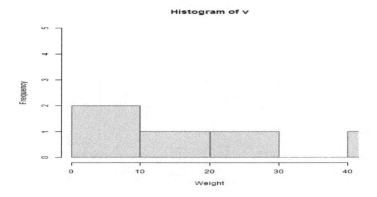

R - Line Graphs

A line chart is a graph that connects a series of points by drawing line segments between them. These points are ordered in one of their coordinate (usually the x-coordinate) value. Line charts are usually used in identifying the trends in data.

The **plot()** function in R is used to create the line graph.

Syntax

The basic syntax to create a line chart in R is −

```
plot(v,type,col,xlab,ylab)
```

Following is the description of the parameters used −

- **v** is a vector containing the numeric values.
- **type** takes the value "p" to draw only the points, "l" to draw only the lines and "o" to draw both points and lines.
- **xlab** is the label for x axis.
- **ylab** is the label for y axis.
- **main** is the Title of the chart.
- **col** is used to give colors to both the points and lines.

Example

A simple line chart is created using the input vector and the type parameter as "O". The below script will create and save a line chart in the current R working directory.

```
# Create the data for the chart.
v <- c(7,12,28,3,41)

# Give the chart file a name.
png(file = "line_chart.jpg")

# Plot the bar chart.
plot(v,type = "o")

# Save the file.
dev.off()
```

When we execute the above code, it produces the following result –

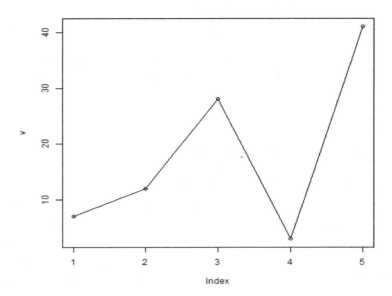

Line Chart Title, Color and Labels:

The features of the line chart can be expanded by using additional parameters. We add color to the points and lines, give a title to the chart and add labels to the axes.

Example:

```
# Create the data for the chart.
v <- c(7,12,28,3,41)

# Give the chart file a name.
png(file = "line_chart_label_colored.jpg")

# Plot the bar chart.
plot(v,type = "o", col = "red", xlab = "Month", ylab = "Rain fall",
   main = "Rain fall chart")

# Save the file.
dev.off()
```

When we execute the above code, it produces the following result –

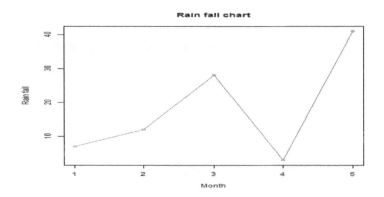

Multiple Lines in a Line Chart:

More than one line can be drawn on the same chart by using the **lines()**function.

After the first line is plotted, the lines() function can use an additional vector as input to draw the second line in the chart,

```
# Create the data for the chart.
v <- c(7,12,28,3,41)
t <- c(14,7,6,19,3)

# Give the chart file a name.
png(file = "line_chart_2_lines.jpg")

# Plot the bar chart.
plot(v,type = "o",col = "red", xlab = "Month", ylab = "Rain fall",
   main = "Rain fall chart")

lines(t, type = "o", col = "blue")

# Save the file.
dev.off()
```

When we execute the above code, it produces the following result –

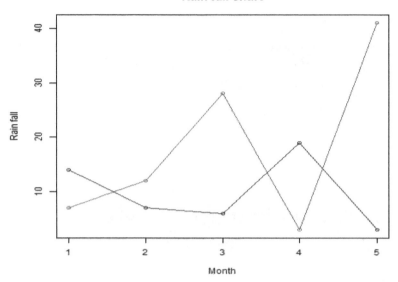

R - Scatterplots

Scatterplots show many points plotted in the Cartesian plane. Each point represents the values of two variables. One variable is chosen in the horizontal axis and another in the vertical axis.

The simple scatterplot is created using the **plot()** function.

Syntax:

The basic syntax for creating scatterplot in R is −

```
plot(x, y, main, xlab, ylab, xlim, ylim, axes)
```

Following is the description of the parameters used −

- **x** is the data set whose values are the horizontal coordinates.

- **y** is the data set whose values are the vertical coordinates.

- **main** is the tile of the graph.

- **xlab** is the label in the horizontal axis.

- **ylab** is the label in the vertical axis.

- **xlim** is the limits of the values of x used for plotting.

- **ylim** is the limits of the values of y used for plotting.

- **axes** indicates whether both axes should be drawn on the plot.

Example

We use the data set **"mtcars"** available in the R environment to create a basic scatterplot. Let's use the columns "wt" and "mpg" in mtcars.

```
input <- mtcars[,c('wt','mpg')]
print(head(input))
```

When we execute the above code, it produces the following result −

```
                  wt    mpg
Mazda RX4         2.620  21.0
Mazda RX4 Wag     2.875  21.0
Datsun 710        2.320  22.8
Hornet 4 Drive    3.215  21.4
Hornet Sportabout 3.440  18.7
Valiant           3.460  18.1
```

Creating the Scatterplot:

The below script will create a scatterplot graph for the relation between wt(weight) and mpg(miles per gallon).

```
# Get the input values.
input <- mtcars[,c('wt','mpg')]

# Give the chart file a name.
png(file = "scatterplot.png")

# Plot the chart for cars with weight between 2.5 to 5 and
mileage between 15 and 30.
plot(x = input$wt,y = input$mpg,
  xlab = "Weight",
```

```
ylab = "Milage",
xlim = c(2.5,5),
ylim = c(15,30),
main = "Weight vs Milage"
)

# Save the file.
dev.off()
```

When we execute the above code, it produces the following result –

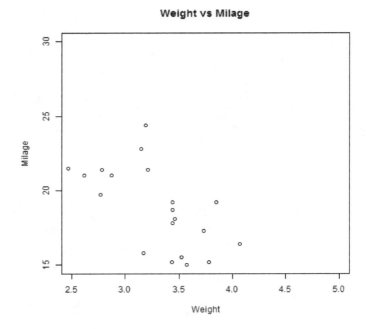

Scatterplot Matrices:

When we have more than two variables and we want to find the correlation between one variable versus the remaining ones we use scatterplot matrix. We use **pairs()**function to create matrices of scatterplots.

Syntax:

The basic syntax for creating scatterplot matrices in R is –

pairs(formula, data)

Following is the description of the parameters used –

- **formula** represents the series of variables used in pairs.

- **data** represents the data set from which the variables will be taken.

Example

Each variable is paired up with each of the remaining variable. A scatterplot is plotted for each pair.

```
# Give the chart file a name.
png(file = "scatterplot_matrices.png")

# Plot the matrices between 4 variables giving 12 plots.

# One variable with 3 others and total 4 variables.

pairs(~wt+mpg+disp+cyl,data = mtcars,
   main = "Scatterplot Matrix")

# Save the file.
dev.off()
```

When the above code is executed we get the following output.

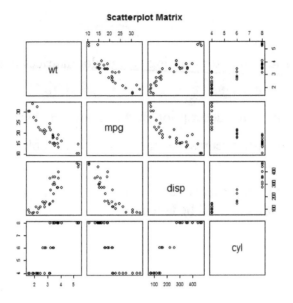

R Programming Statistics Examples

In the next coming chapters, we will learn the basics of statistical inference in order to understand and compute p-values and confidence intervals, all while analyzing data with R. We will provide R programming examples in a way that will help make the connection between concepts and implementation. Problem sets requiring R programming will be used to test understanding and ability to implement basic data analyses. We will use visualization techniques to explore new data sets and determine the most appropriate approach. We will describe robust statistical techniques as alternatives when data do not fit assumptions required by the standard approaches. By using R scripts to analyze data, you will learn the basics of conducting reproducible research.

R - Mean, Median and Mode

Statistical analysis in R is performed by using many in-built functions. Most of these functions are part of the R base package. These functions take R vector as an input along with the arguments and give the result.

The functions we are discussing in this chapter are mean, median and mode.

Mean:

It is calculated by taking the sum of the values and dividing with the number of values in a data series.

The function **mean()** is used to calculate this in R.

Syntax

The basic syntax for calculating mean in R is −

```
mean(x, trim = 0, na.rm = FALSE, ...)
```

Following is the description of the parameters used −

- **x** is the input vector.

- **trim** is used to drop some observations from both end of the sorted vector.

- **na.rm** is used to remove the missing values from the input vector.

Example

```
# Create a vector.
x <- c(12,7,3,4.2,18,2,54,-21,8,-5)

# Find Mean.
result.mean <- mean(x)
print(result.mean)
```

When we execute the above code, it produces the following result −

```
[1] 8.22
```

Applying Trim Option

When trim parameter is supplied, the values in the vector get sorted and then the required numbers of observations are dropped from calculating the mean.

When trim = 0.3, 3 values from each end will be dropped from the calculations to find mean.

In this case the sorted vector is (−21, −5, 2, 3, 4.2, 7, 8, 12, 18, 54) and the values removed from the vector for calculating mean are (−21,−5,2) from left and (12,18,54) from right.

```
# Create a vector.
x <- c(12,7,3,4.2,18,2,54,-21,8,-5)

# Find Mean.
result.mean <- mean(x,trim = 0.3)
```

```
print(result.mean)
```

When we execute the above code, it produces the following result −

```
[1] 5.55
```

Applying NA Option

If there are missing values, then the mean function returns NA.

To drop the missing values from the calculation use na.rm = TRUE. which means remove the NA values.

```
# Create a vector.
x <- c(12,7,3,4.2,18,2,54,-21,8,-5,NA)

# Find mean.
result.mean <- mean(x)
print(result.mean)

# Find mean dropping NA values.
result.mean <- mean(x,na.rm = TRUE)
print(result.mean)
```

When we execute the above code, it produces the following result −

```
[1] NA
[1] 8.22
```

Median:

The middle most value in a data series is called the median. The **median()** function is used in R to calculate this value.

Syntax:

The basic syntax for calculating median in R is −

```
median(x, na.rm = FALSE)
```

Following is the description of the parameters used −

- **x** is the input vector.

- **na.rm** is used to remove the missing values from the input vector.

Example:

```
# Create the vector.
x <- c(12,7,3,4.2,18,2,54,-21,8,-5)

# Find the median.
median.result <- median(x)
print(median.result)
```

When we execute the above code, it produces the following result −

```
[1] 5.6
```

Mode:

The mode is the value that has highest number of occurrences in a set of data. Unike mean and median, mode can have both numeric and character data.

R does not have a standard in-built function to calculate mode. So we create a user function to calculate mode of a data set in R. This function takes the vector as input and gives the mode value as output.

Example:

```
# Create the function.
getmode <- function(v) {
   uniqv <- unique(v)
   uniqv[which.max(tabulate(match(v, uniqv)))]
}

# Create the vector with numbers.
v <- c(2,1,2,3,1,2,3,4,1,5,5,3,2,3)

# Calculate the mode using the user function.
result <- getmode(v)
print(result)

# Create the vector with characters.
charv <- c("o","it","the","it","it")

# Calculate the mode using the user function.
result <- getmode(charv)
print(result)
```

When we execute the above code, it produces the following result −

```
[1] 2
[1] "it"
```

R - Linear Regression

Regression analysis is a very widely used statistical tool to establish a relationship model between two variables. One of these variable is called predictor variable whose value is gathered through experiments. The other variable is called response variable whose value is derived from the predictor variable.

In Linear Regression these two variables are related through an equation, where exponent (power) of both these variables is 1. Mathematically a linear relationship represents a straight line when plotted as a graph. A non-linear relationship where the exponent of any variable is not equal to 1 creates a curve.

The general mathematical equation for a linear regression is −

$$y = ax + b$$

Following is the description of the parameters used −

- **y** is the response variable.

- **x** is the predictor variable.

- **a** and **b** are constants which are called the coefficients.

Steps to Establish a Regression:

A simple example of regression is predicting weight of a person when his height is known. To do this we need to have the relationship between height and weight of a person.

The steps to create the relationship is −

- Carry out the experiment of gathering a sample of observed values of height and corresponding weight.

- Create a relationship model using the **lm()** functions in R.

- Find the coefficients from the model created and create the mathematical equation using these

- Get a summary of the relationship model to know the average error in prediction. Also called **residuals**.

- To predict the weight of new persons, use the **predict()** function in R.

Input Data:

Below is the sample data representing the observations −

Values of height
151, 174, 138, 186, 128, 136, 179, 163, 152, 131

Values of weight.
63, 81, 56, 91, 47, 57, 76, 72, 62, 48

lm() Function:

This function creates the relationship model between the predictor and the response variable.

Syntax:

The basic syntax for **lm()** function in linear regression is −

```
lm(formula,data)
```

Following is the description of the parameters used –

- **formula** is a symbol presenting the relation between x and y.

- **data** is the vector on which the formula will be applied.

Create Relationship Model & get the Coefficients

```
x <- c(151, 174, 138, 186, 128, 136, 179, 163, 152, 131)
y <- c(63, 81, 56, 91, 47, 57, 76, 72, 62, 48)

# Apply the lm() function.
relation <- lm(y~x)

print(relation)
```

When we execute the above code, it produces the following result –

```
Call:
lm(formula = y ~ x)

Coefficients:
(Intercept)        x
  -38.4551      0.6746
```

Get the Summary of the Relationship:

```
x <- c(151, 174, 138, 186, 128, 136, 179, 163, 152, 131)
y <- c(63, 81, 56, 91, 47, 57, 76, 72, 62, 48)
```

```
# Apply the lm() function.
relation <- lm(y~x)

print(summary(relation))
```

When we execute the above code, it produces the following result –

```
Call:
lm(formula = y ~ x)

Residuals:
   Min      1Q   Median     3Q     Max
-6.3002  -1.6629  0.0412  1.8944  3.9775

Coefficients:
          Estimate Std. Error t value Pr(>|t|)
(Intercept) -38.45509   8.04901  -4.778  0.00139 **
x             0.67461   0.05191  12.997 1.16e-06 ***
---
Signif. codes:  0 '***' 0.001 '**' 0.01 '*' 0.05 '.' 0.1 ' ' 1

Residual standard error: 3.253 on 8 degrees of freedom
Multiple R-squared:  0.9548,     Adjusted R-squared: 0.9491
F-statistic: 168.9 on 1 and 8 DF,  p-value: 1.164e-06
```

predict() Function:

Syntax:

The basic syntax for predict() in linear regression is −

predict(object, newdata)

Following is the description of the parameters used −

- **object** is the formula which is already created using the lm() function.

- **newdata** is the vector containing the new value for predictor variable.

Predict the weight of new persons

```
# The predictor vector.
x <- c(151, 174, 138, 186, 128, 136, 179, 163, 152, 131)

# The resposne vector.
y <- c(63, 81, 56, 91, 47, 57, 76, 72, 62, 48)

# Apply the lm() function.
relation <- lm(y~x)

# Find weight of a person with height 170.
a <- data.frame(x = 170)
result <- predict(relation,a)
print(result)
```

When we execute the above code, it produces the following result −

```
       1
76.22869
```

Visualize the Regression Graphically

```
# Create the predictor and response variable.
x <- c(151, 174, 138, 186, 128, 136, 179, 163, 152, 131)
y <- c(63, 81, 56, 91, 47, 57, 76, 72, 62, 48)
relation <- lm(y~x)

# Give the chart file a name.
png(file = "linearregression.png")

# Plot the chart.
plot(y,x,col  =  "blue",main  =  "Height  &  Weight
Regression",
abline(lm(x~y)),cex  =  1.3,pch  =  16,xlab  =  "Weight in
Kg",ylab = "Height in cm")

# Save the file.
dev.off()
```

When we execute the above code, it produces the following result −

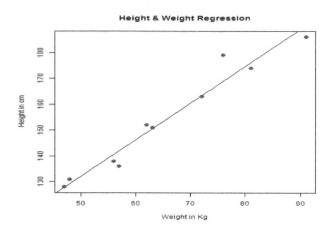

R - Multiple Regression

Multiple regression is an extension of linear regression into relationship between more than two variables. In simple linear relation we have one predictor and one response variable, but in multiple regression we have more than one predictor variable and one response variable.

The general mathematical equation for multiple regression is –

```
y = a + b1x1 + b2x2 +...bnxn
```

Following is the description of the parameters used –

- **y** is the response variable.

- **a, b1, b2...bn** are the coefficients.

- **x1, x2, ...xn** are the predictor variables.

We create the regression model using the **lm()** function in R. The model determines the value of the coefficients using the input data. Next we can predict the value of the response variable for a given set of predictor variables using these coefficients.

lm() Function:

This function creates the relationship model between the predictor and the response variable.

Syntax:

The basic syntax for **lm()** function in multiple regression is –

```
lm(y ~ x1+x2+x3...,data)
```

Following is the description of the parameters used –

- **formula** is a symbol presenting the relation between the response variable and predictor variables.

- **data** is the vector on which the formula will be applied.

Examples:

Input Data:

Consider the data set "mtcars" available in the R environment. It gives a comparison between different car models in terms of mileage per gallon (mpg), cylinder displacement("disp"), horse power("hp"), weight of the car("wt") and some more parameters.

The goal of the model is to establish the relationship between "mpg" as a response variable with "disp","hp" and "wt" as predictor variables. We create a subset of these variables from the mtcars data set for this purpose.

```
input <- mtcars[,c("mpg","disp","hp","wt")]
print(head(input))
```

When we execute the above code, it produces the following result –

```
                   mpg  disp hp   wt
Mazda RX4          21.0 160  110  2.620
Mazda RX4 Wag      21.0 160  110  2.875
Datsun 710         22.8 108  93   2.320
Hornet 4 Drive     21.4 258  110  3.215
Hornet Sportabout  18.7 360  175  3.440
Valiant            18.1 225  105  3.460
```

Create Relationship Model & get the Coefficients

```
input <- mtcars[,c("mpg","disp","hp","wt")]

# Create the relationship model.
model <- lm(mpg~disp+hp+wt, data = input)

# Show the model.
print(model)

# Get the Intercept and coefficients as vector elements.
cat("# # # # The Coefficient Values # # # ","\n")

a <- coef(model)[1]
print(a)

Xdisp <- coef(model)[2]
Xhp <- coef(model)[3]
Xwt <- coef(model)[4]

print(Xdisp)
print(Xhp)
print(Xwt)
```

When we execute the above code, it produces the following result −

```
Call:
lm(formula = mpg ~ disp + hp + wt, data = input)

Coefficients:
(Intercept)      disp         hp          wt
  37.105505    -0.000937    -0.031157    -3.800891
```

```
# # # # The Coefficient Values # # #
(Intercept)
  37.10551
     disp
-0.0009370091
     hp
-0.03115655
     wt
-3.800891
```

Create Equation for Regression Model:

Based on the above intercept and coefficient values, we create the mathematical equation.

```
Y = a+Xdisp.x1+Xhp.x2+Xwt.x3
or
Y = 37.15+(-0.000937)*x1+(-0.0311)*x2+(-3.8008)*x3
```

Apply Equation for predicting New Values:

We can use the regression equation created above to predict the mileage when a new set of values for displacement, horse power and weight is provided.

For a car with disp = 221, hp = 102 and wt = 2.91 the predicted mileage is –

```
Y    =    37.15+(-0.000937)*221+(-0.0311)*102+(-3.8008)*2.91 = 22.7104
```

R - Logistic Regression

The Logistic Regression is a regression model in which the response variable (dependent variable) has categorical values such as True/False or 0/1. It actually measures the probability of a binary response as the value of response variable based on the mathematical equation relating it with the predictor variables.

The general mathematical equation for logistic regression is −

y = 1/(1+e^-(a+b1x1+b2x2+b3x3+...))

Following is the description of the parameters used −

- **y** is the response variable.

- **x** is the predictor variable.

- **a** and **b** are the coefficients which are numeric constants.

The function used to create the regression model is the **glm()** function.

Syntax:

The basic syntax for **glm()** function in logistic regression is −

glm(formula,data,family)

Following is the description of the parameters used −

- **formula** is the symbol presenting the relationship between the variables.

- **data** is the data set giving the values of these variables.

- **family** is R object to specify the details of the model. It's value is binomial for logistic regression.

Example

The in-built data set "mtcars" describes different models of a car with their various engine specifications. In "mtcars" data set, the transmission mode (automatic or manual) is described by the column am which is a binary value (0 or 1). We can create a logistic regression model between the columns "am" and 3 other columns - hp, wt and cyl.

```
# Select some columns form mtcars.
input <- mtcars[,c("am","cyl","hp","wt")]

print(head(input))
```

When we execute the above code, it produces the following result −

```
                  am  cyl  hp   wt
Mazda RX4          1   6   110  2.620
Mazda RX4 Wag      1   6   110  2.875
Datsun 710         1   4   93   2.320
Hornet 4 Drive     0   6   110  3.215
Hornet Sportabout  0   8   175  3.440
Valiant            0   6   105  3.460
```

Create Regression Model:

We use the **glm()** function to create the regression model and get its summary for analysis.

```
input <- mtcars[,c("am","cyl","hp","wt")]

am.data = glm(formula = am ~ cyl + hp + wt, data = input,
family = binomial)

print(summary(am.data))
```

When we execute the above code, it produces the following result −

```
Call:
glm(formula = am ~ cyl + hp + wt, family = binomial, data
= input)

Deviance Residuals:
   Min      1Q    Median      3Q      Max
-2.17272  -0.14907 -0.01464   0.14116  1.27641

Coefficients:
            Estimate Std. Error z value Pr(>|z|)
(Intercept) 19.70288   8.11637   2.428   0.0152 *
cyl          0.48760   1.07162   0.455   0.6491
hp           0.03259   0.01886   1.728   0.0840 .
wt          -9.14947   4.15332  -2.203   0.0276 *
---
Signif. codes:  0 '***' 0.001 '**' 0.01 '*' 0.05 '.' 0.1 ' ' 1
```

(Dispersion parameter for binomial family taken to be 1)

  Null deviance: 43.2297 on 31 degrees of freedom
Residual deviance: 9.8415 on 28 degrees of freedom
AIC: 17.841

Number of Fisher Scoring iterations: 8

Conclusion:

In the summary as the p-value in the last column is more than 0.05 for the variables "cyl" and "hp", we consider them to be insignificant in contributing to the value of the variable "am". Only weight (wt) impacts the "am" value in this regression model.

R - Normal Distribution

In a random collection of data from independent sources, it is generally observed that the distribution of data is normal. Which means, on plotting a graph with the value of the variable in the horizontal axis and the count of the values in the vertical axis we get a bell shape curve. The center of the curve represents the mean of the data set. In the graph, fifty percent of values lie to the left of the mean and the other fifty percent lie to the right of the graph. This is referred as normal distribution in statistics.

R has four in built functions to generate normal distribution. They are described below.

dnorm(x, mean, sd)
pnorm(x, mean, sd)
qnorm(p, mean, sd)
rnorm(n, mean, sd)

Following is the description of the parameters used in above functions –

- **x** is a vector of numbers.

- **p** is a vector of probabilities.

- **n** is number of observations(sample size).

- **mean** is the mean value of the sample data. It's default value is zero.

- **sd** is the standard deviation. It's default value is 1.

dnorm()

This function gives height of the probability distribution at each point for a given mean and standard deviation.

```
# Create a sequence of numbers between -10 and 10
incrementing by 0.1.
x <- seq(-10, 10, by = .1)

# Choose the mean as 2.5 and standard deviation as 0.5.
y <- dnorm(x, mean = 2.5, sd = 0.5)

# Give the chart file a name.
png(file = "dnorm.png")

plot(x,y)

# Save the file.
dev.off()
```

When we execute the above code, it produces the following result −

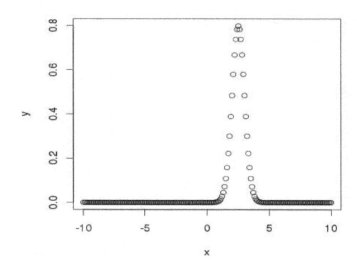

pnorm()

This function gives the probability of a normally distributed random number to be less that the value of a given number. It is also called "Cumulative Distribution Function".

```
# Create a sequence of numbers between -10 and 10
incrementing by 0.2.
x <- seq(-10,10,by = .2)

# Choose the mean as 2.5 and standard deviation as 2.
y <- pnorm(x, mean = 2.5, sd = 2)

# Give the chart file a name.
png(file = "pnorm.png")

# Plot the graph.
plot(x,y)

# Save the file.
dev.off()
```

When we execute the above code, it produces the following result −

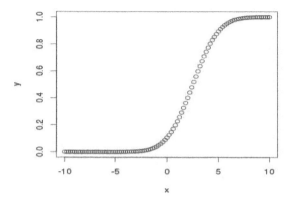

qnorm()

This function takes the probability value and gives a number whose cumulative value matches the probability value.

```
# Create a sequence of probability values incrementing by
0.02.
x <- seq(0, 1, by = 0.02)

# Choose the mean as 2 and standard deviation as 3.
y <- qnorm(x, mean = 2, sd = 1)

# Give the chart file a name.
png(file = "qnorm.png")

# Plot the graph.
plot(x,y)

# Save the file.
dev.off()
```

When we execute the above code, it produces the following result −

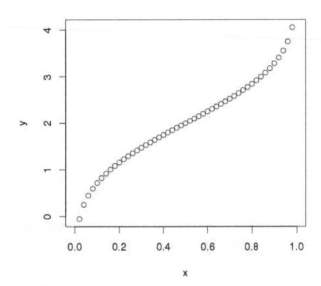

rnorm()

This function is used to generate random numbers whose distribution is normal. It takes the sample size as input and generates that many random numbers. We draw a histogram to show the distribution of the generated numbers.

```
# Create a sample of 50 numbers which are normally
distributed.
y <- rnorm(50)

# Give the chart file a name.
```

```
png(file = "rnorm.png")

# Plot the histogram for this sample.
hist(y, main = "Normal DIstribution")

# Save the file.
dev.off()
```

When we execute the above code, it produces the following result −

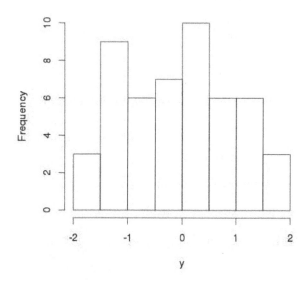

Normal DIstribution

R - Binomial Distribution

The binomial distribution model deals with finding the probability of success of an event which has only two possible outcomes in a series of experiments. For example, tossing of a coin always gives a head or a tail. The probability of finding exactly 3 heads in tossing a coin repeatedly for 10 times is estimated during the binomial distribution.

R has four in-built functions to generate binomial distribution. They are described below.

dbinom(x, size, prob)
pbinom(x, size, prob)
qbinom(p, size, prob)
rbinom(n, size, prob)

Following is the description of the parameters used –

- **x** is a vector of numbers.

- **p** is a vector of probabilities.

- **n** is number of observations.

- **size** is the number of trials.

- **prob** is the probability of success of each trial.

dbinom()

This function gives the probability density distribution at each point.

```
# Create a sample of 50 numbers which are incremented by
1.
x <- seq(0,50,by = 1)

# Create the binomial distribution.
y <- dbinom(x,50,0.5)

# Give the chart file a name.
png(file = "dbinom.png")

# Plot the graph for this sample.
plot(x,y)

# Save the file.
dev.off()
```

When we execute the above code, it produces the
following result −

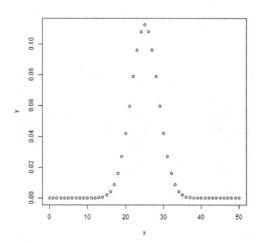

pbinom()

This function gives the cumulative probability of an event. It is a single value representing the probability.

```
# Probability of getting 26 or less heads from a 51 tosses of
a coin.
x <- pbinom(26,51,0.5)

print(x)
```

When we execute the above code, it produces the following result −

```
[1] 0.610116
```

qbinom()

This function takes the probability value and gives a number whose cumulative value matches the probability value.

```
# How many heads will have a probability of 0.25 will
come out when a coin
# is tossed 51 times.
x <- qbinom(0.25,51,1/2)

print(x)
```

When we execute the above code, it produces the following result −

```
[1] 23
```

rbinom()

This function generates required number of random values of given probability from a given sample.

```
# Find 8 random values from a sample of 150 with
probability of 0.4.
x <- rbinom(8,150,.4)

print(x)
```

When we execute the above code, it produces the following result –

```
[1] 58 61 59 66 55 60 61 67
```

R - Poisson Regression

Poisson Regression involves regression models in which the response variable is in the form of counts and not fractional numbers. For example, the count of number of births or number of wins in a football match series. Also the values of the response variables follow a Poisson distribution.

The general mathematical equation for Poisson regression is −

```
log(y) = a + b1x1 + b2x2 + bnxn.....
```

Following is the description of the parameters used −

- **y** is the response variable.
- **a** and **b** are the numeric coefficients.
- **x** is the predictor variable.

The function used to create the Poisson regression model is the **glm()** function.

Syntax

The basic syntax for **glm()** function in Poisson regression is −

```
glm(formula,data,family)
```

Following is the description of the parameters used in above functions −

- **formula** is the symbol presenting the relationship between the variables.
- **data** is the data set giving the values of these variables.

- **family** is R object to specify the details of the model. It's value is 'Poisson' for Logistic Regression.

Example:

We have the in-built data set "warpbreaks" which describes the effect of wool type (A or B) and tension (low, medium or high) on the number of warp breaks per loom. Let's consider "breaks" as the response variable which is a count of number of breaks. The wool "type" and "tension" are taken as predictor variables.

Input Data

```
input <- warpbreaks
print(head(input))
```

When we execute the above code, it produces the following result –

	breaks	wool	tension
1	26	A	L
2	30	A	L
3	54	A	L
4	25	A	L
5	70	A	L
6	52	A	L

Create Regression Model:

```
output <-glm(formula = breaks ~ wool+tension, data = warpbreaks,
   family = poisson)
print(summary(output))
```

When we execute the above code, it produces the following result –

```
Call:
glm(formula = breaks ~ wool + tension, family = poisson,
data = warpbreaks)

Deviance Residuals:
  Min    1Q    Median    3Q    Max
-3.6871 -1.6503 -0.4269  1.1902  4.2616

Coefficients:
          Estimate Std. Error z value Pr(>|z|)
(Intercept)  3.69196   0.04541  81.302  < 2e-16 ***
woolB       -0.20599   0.05157  -3.994 6.49e-05 ***
tensionM    -0.32132   0.06027  -5.332 9.73e-08 ***
tensionH    -0.51849   0.06396  -8.107 5.21e-16 ***
---
Signif. codes:  0 '***' 0.001 '**' 0.01 '*' 0.05 '.' 0.1 ' ' 1

(Dispersion parameter for poisson family taken to be 1)

    Null deviance: 297.37  on 53  degrees of freedom
Residual deviance: 210.39  on 50  degrees of freedom
```

AIC: 493.06

Number of Fisher Scoring iterations: 4

In the summary we look for the p-value in the last column to be less than 0.05 to consider an impact of the predictor variable on the response variable. As seen the wooltype B having tension type M and H have impact on the count of breaks.

R - Analysis of Covariance

We use Regression analysis to create models which describe the effect of variation in predictor variables on the response variable. Sometimes, if we have a categorical variable with values like Yes/No or Male/Female etc. The simple regression analysis gives multiple results for each value of the categorical variable. In such scenario, we can study the effect of the categorical variable by using it along with the predictor variable and comparing the regression lines for each level of the categorical variable. Such an analysis is termed as **Analysis of Covariance** also called as **ANCOVA**.

Example

Consider the R built in data set mtcars. In it we observer that the field "am" represents the type of transmission (auto or manual). It is a categorical variable with values 0 and 1. The miles per gallon value(mpg) of a car can also depend on it besides the value of horse power("hp").

We study the effect of the value of "am" on the regression between "mpg" and "hp". It is done by using the **aov()** function followed by the **anova()** function to compare the multiple regressions.

Input Data:

Create a data frame containing the fields "mpg", "hp" and "am" from the data set mtcars. Here we take "mpg" as the response variable, "hp" as the predictor variable and "am" as the categorical variable.

```
input <- mtcars[,c("am","mpg","hp")]
print(head(input))
```

When we execute the above code, it produces the following result –

```
                   am mpg   hp
Mazda RX4           1  21.0 110
Mazda RX4 Wag       1  21.0 110
Datsun 710          1  22.8  93
Hornet 4 Drive      0  21.4 110
Hornet Sportabout   0  18.7 175
Valiant             0  18.1 105
```

ANCOVA Analysis:

We create a regression model taking "hp" as the predictor variable and "mpg" as the response variable taking into account the interaction between "am" and "hp".

Model with interaction between categorical variable and predictor variable

```
# Get the dataset.
input <- mtcars

# Create the regression model.
result <- aov(mpg~hp*am,data = input)
print(summary(result))
```

When we execute the above code, it produces the following result –

```
         Df Sum Sq Mean Sq F value  Pr(>F)
hp        1 678.4  678.4 77.391 1.50e-09 ***
am        1 202.2  202.2 23.072 4.75e-05 ***
hp:am     1  0.0    0.0  0.001   0.981
Residuals 28 245.4  8.8
---
Signif. codes:  0 '***' 0.001 '**' 0.01 '*' 0.05 '.' 0.1 ' ' 1
```

This result shows that both horse power and transmission type has significant effect on miles per gallon as the p value in both cases is less than 0.05. But the interaction between these two variables is not significant as the p-value is more than 0.05.

Model without interaction between categorical variable and predictor variable:

```
# Get the dataset.
input <- mtcars

# Create the regression model.
result <- aov(mpg~hp+am,data = input)
print(summary(result))
```

When we execute the above code, it produces the following result –

```
         Df Sum Sq Mean Sq  F value  Pr(>F)
hp        1 678.4  678.4  80.15 7.63e-10 ***
am        1 202.2  202.2  23.89 3.46e-05 ***
```

```
Residuals  29 245.4   8.5
---
Signif. codes:  0 '***' 0.001 '**' 0.01 '*' 0.05 '.' 0.1 ' ' 1
```

This result shows that both horse power and transmission type has significant effect on miles per gallon as the p value in both cases is less than 0.05.

Comparing Two Models:

Now we can compare the two models to conclude if the interaction of the variables is truly in-significant. For this we use the **anova()** function.

```
# Get the dataset.
input <- mtcars

# Create the regression models.
result1 <- aov(mpg~hp*am,data = input)
result2 <- aov(mpg~hp+am,data = input)

# Compare the two models.
print(anova(result1,result2))
```

When we execute the above code, it produces the following result −

```
Model 1: mpg ~ hp * am
Model 2: mpg ~ hp + am
  Res.Df   RSS Df  Sum of Sq    F Pr(>F)
1    28 245.43
2    29 245.44 -1 -0.0052515 6e-04 0.9806
```

As the p-value is greater than 0.05 we conclude that the interaction between horse power and transmission type is not significant. So the mileage per gallon will depend in a similar manner on the horse power of the car in both auto and manual transmission mode.

R - Time Series Analysis

Time series is a series of data points in which each data point is associated with a timestamp. A simple example is the price of a stock in the stock market at different points of time on a given day. Another example is the amount of rainfall in a region at different months of the year. R language uses many functions to create, manipulate and plot the time series data. The data for the time series is stored in an R object called **time-series object**. It is also a R data object like a vector or data frame.

The time series object is created by using the **ts()** function.

Syntax:

The basic syntax for **ts()** function in time series analysis is −

timeseries.object.name <- ts(data, start, end, frequency)

Following is the description of the parameters used −

- **data** is a vector or matrix containing the values used in the time series.

- **start** specifies the start time for the first observation in time series.

- **end** specifies the end time for the last observation in time series.

- **frequency** specifies the number of observations per unit time.

Except the parameter "data" all other parameters are optional.

Example:

Consider the annual rainfall details at a place starting from January 2012. We create an R time series object for a period of 12 months and plot it.

```
# Get the data points in form of a R vector.
rainfall                                        <-
c(799,1174.8,865.1,1334.6,635.4,918.5,685.5,998.6,784.2,
985,882.8,1071)

# Convert it to a time series object.
rainfall.timeseries <- ts(rainfall,start = c(2012,1),frequency
= 12)

# Print the timeseries data.
print(rainfall.timeseries)

# Give the chart file a name.
png(file = "rainfall.png")

# Plot a graph of the time series.
plot(rainfall.timeseries)

# Save the file.
dev.off()
```

When we execute the above code, it produces the following result and chart –

```
Jan   Feb   Mar   Apr   May    Jun   Jul   Aug   Sep
2012  799.0  1174.8  865.1  1334.6  635.4  918.5  685.5
998.6  784.2
      Oct   Nov   Dec
2012  985.0  882.8  1071.0
```

The Time series chart:

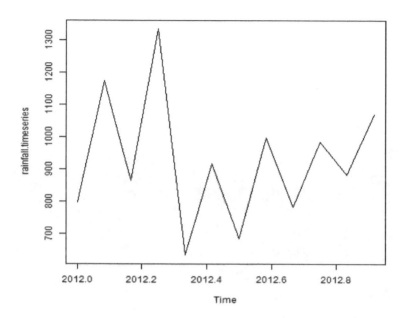

Different Time Intervals:

The value of the **frequency** parameter in the ts() function decides the time intervals at which the data points are measured. A value of 12 indicates that the time series is for 12 months. Other values and its meaning is as below –

- **frequency** = **12** pegs the data points for every month of a year.

- **frequency** = **4** pegs the data points for every quarter of a year.

- **frequency** = **6** pegs the data points for every 10 minutes of an hour.

- **frequency = 24*6** pegs the data points for every 10 minutes of a day.

Multiple Time Series

We can plot multiple time series in one chart by combining both the series into a matrix.

```
# Get the data points in form of a R vector.
rainfall1                                              <-
c(799,1174.8,865.1,1334.6,635.4,918.5,685.5,998.6,784.2,
985,882.8,1071)
rainfall2 <-

c(655,1306.9,1323.4,1172.2,562.2,824,822.4,1265.5,799.6,
1105.6,1106.7,1337.8)

# Convert them to a matrix.
combined.rainfall  <-  matrix(c(rainfall1,rainfall2),nrow =
12)

# Convert it to a time series object.
rainfall.timeseries      <-     ts(combined.rainfall,start   =
c(2012,1),frequency = 12)

# Print the timeseries data.
print(rainfall.timeseries)

# Give the chart file a name.
png(file = "rainfall_combined.png")

# Plot a graph of the time series.
```

```
plot(rainfall.timeseries, main = "Multiple Time Series")

# Save the file.
dev.off()
```

When we execute the above code, it produces the following result and chart −

	Series 1	Series 2
Jan 2012	799.0	655.0
Feb 2012	1174.8	1306.9
Mar 2012	865.1	1323.4
Apr 2012	1334.6	1172.2
May 2012	635.4	562.2
Jun 2012	918.5	824.0
Jul 2012	685.5	822.4
Aug 2012	998.6	1265.5
Sep 2012	784.2	799.6
Oct 2012	985.0	1105.6
Nov 2012	882.8	1106.7
Dec 2012	1071.0	1337.8

The Multiple Time series chart:

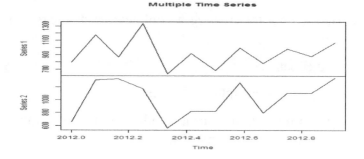

R - Nonlinear Least Square

When modeling real world data for regression analysis, we observe that it is rarely the case that the equation of the model is a linear equation giving a linear graph. Most of the time, the equation of the model of real world data involves mathematical functions of higher degree like an exponent of 3 or a sin function. In such a scenario, the plot of the model gives a curve rather than a line. The goal of both linear and non-linear regression is to adjust the values of the model's parameters to find the line or curve that comes closest to your data. On finding these values we will be able to estimate the response variable with good accuracy.

In Least Square regression, we establish a regression model in which the sum of the squares of the vertical distances of different points from the regression curve is minimized. We generally start with a defined model and assume some values for the coefficients. We then apply the **nls()** function of R to get the more accurate values along with the confidence intervals.

Syntax

The basic syntax for creating a nonlinear least square test in R is −

```
nls(formula, data, start)
```

Following is the description of the parameters used −

- **formula** is a nonlinear model formula including variables and parameters.

- **data** is a data frame used to evaluate the variables in the formula.

- **start** is a named list or named numeric vector of starting estimates.

Example:

We will consider a nonlinear model with assumption of initial values of its coefficients. Next we will see what is the confidence intervals of these assumed values so that we can judge how well these values fir into the model.

So let's consider the below equation for this purpose –

a = b1*x^2+b2

Let's assume the initial coefficients to be 1 and 3 and fit these values into nls() function.

```
xvalues <- c(1.6,2.1,2,2.23,3.71,3.25,3.4,3.86,1.19,2.21)
yvalues                                                  <-
c(5.19,7.43,6.94,8.11,18.75,14.88,16.06,19.12,3.21,7.58)

# Give the chart file a name.
png(file = "nls.png")


# Plot these values.
plot(xvalues,yvalues)


# Take the assumed values and fit into the model.
model <- nls(yvalues ~ b1*xvalues^2+b2,start = list(b1 =
1,b2 = 3))

# Plot the chart with new data by fitting it to a prediction
from 100 data points.
```

```
new.data              <-              data.frame(xvalues
seq(min(xvalues),max(xvalues),len = 100))
lines(new.data$xvalues,predict(model,newdata
new.data))

# Save the file.
dev.off()

# Get the sum of the squared residuals.
print(sum(resid(model)^2))

# Get the confidence intervals on the chosen values of the
coefficients.
print(confint(model))
```

When we execute the above code, it produces the following result –

```
[1] 1.081935
Waiting for profiling to be done...
     2.5%   97.5%
b1 1.137708 1.253135
b2 1.497364 2.496484
```

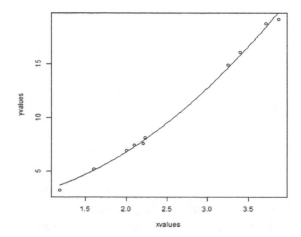

We can conclude that the value of b1 is more close to 1 while the value of b2 is more close to 2 and not 3.

R - Decision Tree

Decision tree is a graph to represent choices and their results in form of a tree. The nodes in the graph represent an event or choice and the edges of the graph represent the decision rules or conditions. It is mostly used in Machine Learning and Data Mining applications using R.

Examples of use of decision tress is – predicting an email as spam or not spam, predicting of a tumor is cancerous or predicting a loan as a good or bad credit risk based on the factors in each of these. Generally, a model is created with observed data also called training data. Then a set of validation data is used to verify and improve the model. R has packages which are used to create and visualize decision trees. For new set of predictor variable, we use this model to arrive at a decision on the category (yes/No, spam/not spam) of the data.

The R package **"party"** is used to create decision trees.

Install R Package

Use the below command in R console to install the package. You also have to install the dependent packages if any.

```
install.packages("party")
```

The package "party" has the function **ctree()** which is used to create and analyze decison tree.

Syntax

The basic syntax for creating a decision tree in R is –

```
ctree(formula, data)
```

Following is the description of the parameters used –

- **formula** is a formula describing the predictor and response variables.

- **data** is the name of the data set used.

Input Data

We will use the R in-built data set named **readingSkills** to create a decision tree. It describes the score of someone's readingSkills if we know the variables "age","shoesize","score" and whether the person is a native speaker or not.

Here is the sample data.

```
# Load the party package. It will automatically load other
# dependent packages.
library(party)

# Print some records from data set readingSkills.
print(head(readingSkills))
```

When we execute the above code, it produces the following result and chart –

```
  nativeSpeaker  age  shoeSize     score
1          yes    5  24.83189  32.29385
2          yes    6  25.95238  36.63105
3           no   11  30.42170  49.60593
4          yes    7  28.66450  40.28456
5          yes   11  31.88207  55.46085
6          yes   10  30.07843  52.83124
Loading required package: methods
Loading required package: grid
```

....
....

Example:

We will use the **ctree()** function to create the decision tree and see its graph.

```
# Load the party package. It will automatically load other
# dependent packages.
library(party)

# Create the input data frame.
input.dat <- readingSkills[c(1:105),]

# Give the chart file a name.
png(file = "decision_tree.png")

# Create the tree.
  output.tree <- ctree(
  nativeSpeaker ~ age + shoeSize + score,
  data = input.dat)

# Plot the tree.
plot(output.tree)

# Save the file.
dev.off()
```

When we execute the above code, it produces the following result −

```
null device
        1
Loading required package: methods
```

Loading required package: grid
Loading required package: mvtnorm
Loading required package: modeltools
Loading required package: stats4
Loading required package: strucchange
Loading required package: zoo

Attaching package: 'zoo'

The following objects are masked from 'package:base':

  as.Date, as.Date.numeric

Loading required package: sandwich

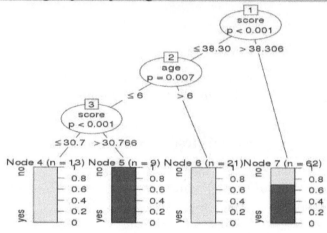

Conclusion

From the decision tree shown above we can conclude that anyone whose readingSkills score is less than 38.3 and age is more than 6 is not a native Speaker.

R - Random Forest

In the random forest approach, a large number of decision trees are created. Every observation is fed into every decision tree. The most common outcome for each observation is used as the final output. A new observation is fed into all the trees and taking a majority vote for each classification model.

An error estimate is made for the cases which were not used while building the tree. That is called an **OOB (Out-of-bag)** error estimate which is mentioned as a percentage.

The R package **"randomForest"** is used to create random forests.

Install R Package

Use the below command in R console to install the package. You also have to install the dependent packages if any.

install.packages("randomForest)

The package "randomForest" has the function **randomForest()** which is used to create and analyze random forests.

Syntax

The basic syntax for creating a random forest in R is −

randomForest(formula, data)

Following is the description of the parameters used −

- **formula** is a formula describing the predictor and response variables.

- **data** is the name of the data set used.

Input Data

We will use the R in-built data set named readingSkills to create a decision tree. It describes the score of someone's readingSkills if we know the variables "age","shoesize","score" and whether the person is a native speaker.

Here is the sample data.

```
# Load the party package. It will automatically load other
# required packages.
library(party)

# Print some records from data set readingSkills.
print(head(readingSkills))
```

When we execute the above code, it produces the following result and chart –

```
  nativeSpeaker  age  shoeSize     score
1          yes    5   24.83189  32.29385
2          yes    6   25.95238  36.63105
3           no   11   30.42170  49.60593
4          yes    7   28.66450  40.28456
5          yes   11   31.88207  55.46085
6          yes   10   30.07843  52.83124
Loading required package: methods
Loading required package: grid
...........................
...........................
```

Example

We will use the **randomForest()** function to create the decision tree and see it's graph.

```
# Load the party package. It will automatically load other
# required packages.
library(party)
library(randomForest)

# Create the forest.
output.forest <- randomForest(nativeSpeaker ~ age +
shoeSize + score,
      data = readingSkills)

# View the forest results.
print(output.forest)

# Importance of each predictor.
print(importance(fit,type = 2))
```

When we execute the above code, it produces the following result −

```
Call:
 randomForest(formula = nativeSpeaker ~ age + shoeSize +
score,
          data = readingSkills)
          Type of random forest: classification
                Number of trees: 500
No. of variables tried at each split: 1

    OOB estimate of error rate: 1%
Confusion matrix:
  no yes class.error
```

```
no  99  1      0.01
yes  1  99     0.01
        MeanDecreaseGini
age          13.95406
shoeSize     18.91006
score        56.73051
```

Conclusion:

From the random forest shown above we can conclude that the shoesize and score are the important factors deciding if someone is a native speaker or not. Also the model has only 1% error which means we can predict with 99% accuracy.

Thank You!

www.ingramcontent.com/pod-product-compliance
Lightning Source LLC
LaVergne TN
LVHW041209050326
832903LV00021B/541